Introducing Engineering in K-8 Settings

Introducing Engineering in K-8 Settings will provide you with the tools you need to incorporate engineering design into your classroom. Rather than prescribing a specific curriculum to follow, this book will help you engage your students with hands-on, open-ended engineering design problems that can be easily integrated into your existing classroom setup.

Beginning with the basics of K-8 engineering, and advancing to topics such as integrating engineering with other disciplines, documentation, and assessments, the chapters provide a how-to on creating open-ended engineering activities, design tasks, and projects that are reflective of the academic, social, emotional, developmental, and community goals of your students. An additional focus is on ways to adapt these pedagogical approaches to meet the needs of all students, representative of racially, ethnically, socioeconomically, and gender diverse populations and students who receive special education services. Case studies and practical implementation strategies are presented alongside more than fifteen lesson plans, with tips on how to modify the tasks presented in the book to work with your classroom and students. This user-centered approach will also help you create your own engineering lessons that meet your individual classroom objectives and interests, and be able to recognize and classify your students' engineering behaviors to support them in enacting their ideas.

No matter your experience or comfort level, this book will be an invaluable resource for elementary and middle school science and technology teachers at all career stages who are looking to introduce engineering design to their students.

Additional classroom resources can be found online at introducingengineering.org.

Elissa Milto is the Director of Outreach at Tufts Center for Engineering Education and Outreach, USA.

Chelsea Andrews is a research assistant professor at Tufts Center for Engineering Education and Outreach, USA.

Merredith Portsmore serves as the Director of Tufts Center for Engineering Education and Outreach and as a research associate professor, USA.

Christopher Wright is an associate professor in the School of Education at Drexel University, USA.

Introducing Engineering in K-8 Settings

Fostering Children's Powerful Design Ideas

Elissa Milto, Chelsea Andrews, Merredith Portsmore, and Christopher Wright

Routledge
Taylor & Francis Group

NEW YORK AND LONDON

Designed cover image: © Steven Andrews

First published 2025
by Routledge
605 Third Avenue, New York, NY 10158

and by Routledge
4 Park Square, Milton Park, Abingdon, Oxon, OX14 4RN

Routledge is an imprint of the Taylor & Francis Group, an informa business

ISBN: 978-1-032-45672-0 (hbk)
ISBN: 978-1-032-42987-8 (pbk)
ISBN: 978-1-003-37817-4 (ebk)

DOI: 10.4324/9781003378174

Typeset in Palatino
by Apex CoVantage, LLC

Access additional resources: introducingengineering.org

Contents

About the Authors

Chelsea Andrews is a research assistant professor at Tufts Center for Engineering Education and Outreach. She has a background in civil and ocean engineering and education. She designs and studies activities, structures, and technologies that support engineering knowledge construction for students and teachers.

Elissa Milto is the Director of Outreach at Tufts Center for Engineering Education and Outreach. After teaching special education, she pursued a degree in STEM education. In her current work, she uses her special education background as she designs engineering education resources and in her work with teachers.

Merredith Portsmore serves as the Director of Tufts Center for Engineering Education and Outreach in addition to being a research professor at the center. She has a background in mechanical engineering and education. She is dedicated to bridging research and practice in both formal and informal engineering education.

Christopher Wright is an associate professor at the School of Education at Drexel University. Prior to engaging in STEM education research, he served as a secondary engineering instructor. His current work focuses on learning and identity development for minoritized youths in engineering contexts.

Preface

Students of all ages should have the opportunity to engage in meaningful work that allows them to incorporate and explore their own ideas. Engineering can give students this chance. As students work through the engineering design process and design solutions to problems, they can also work on a range of skills that will help them become the next generation of problem solvers. Teachers are integral to this process, both in setting up the design challenges and in supporting their students as they work through them.

The authors of this book have been working in pre-college engineering education with educators and students since the mid-1990s. Our backgrounds include social sciences, education (ranging from kindergarten through college), mechanical and civil engineering, special education, and architecture. Some of us have been classroom teachers, while others have researched engineering education and have directly worked with K-8 students in a variety of settings including public and private schools and informal education. We have also worked with teachers as collaborators and have taught classes and led professional development for pre- and in-service teachers.

There is a growing community of engineering education researchers and professionals, and our work is part of this larger community. We wanted to write this book to encourage other educators to do hands-on, open-ended engineering that is inclusive of all students. We also acknowledge that there is a lot to balance as you do this and that this can sometimes be intimidating. Our goal for this book is to share our experiences to help you to grow your understanding of engineering as a discipline and what its inclusion can look like in K-8.

Research and experience demonstrate that children can think deeply about problems and use prior experiences as they design solutions. We value this preexisting student knowledge, and we design activities that encourage students to build upon their prior knowledge about the world, natural and manmade—as they design solutions. For teachers, our core belief is that they need to have flexibility and opportunities to make decisions about their classrooms and their students' learning. We see teachers as capable professionals who do not need "teacher-proof" curricula and believe they should be empowered to design learning environments. Along with this flexibility is the opportunity to listen and respond to students' ideas. When given the freedom to be responsive to student thinking, teachers can make judgments about their students' learning and decide how to support their work. Since our work is student-centered, we see a teacher's role as facilitating learning, discussions, and design learning experiences. Our hope is that this book will help educators understand the engineering young students can do and how to support this work with their own students. While writing this book, we've examined our interactions with teachers and students who have been part of our research, workshops, and classroom interactions. Throughout this book, we will present brief moments of classroom conversations or whole case studies to illustrate what we are talking about.

Acknowledgments

Thank you to all the teachers who supported the authors in research and testing of engineering in their classrooms and settings over the years. Special thanks to Rachel Bandi, Tracy Doyle, Jen Gilbert, Vera Gor, Maggie Jackson, Molly Malinowski, Mary Moran, Erik Murray, Shannon Rausch, Naina Sood-Fox, and Rae Woodcock.

Thank you to all the staff, faculty, collaborators, consultants, graduate students, and post-doctoral fellows who supported or inspired the authors— Linda Beardsley, Suzanne Berryman, Alison Blanchard, Bàrbara Brizuela, Briana Bouchard, Barbara Bratzel, Bill Church, Jennifer Cross, Tejaswini Dalvi, Ethan Danahy, Natalie De Lucca, Milan Dahal, Hoda Ehsan, Alison Earnhart, Brian Gravel, David Hammer, Robert Hayes, John Heffernan, Torben Jessen, Tyrine Jamilla Pangan, Kevin Lavigne, Fatima Rahman, Lisa Meyers, Karen Miel, Matthew Mueller, Greses Pérez, Lynne Ramsey, Chris Rogers, Magee Shalhoub, Dipeshwor Man Shrestha, Isabella Stuopis, Amanda Strawhacker, Chris Swan, Rebecca Swanson, Jessica Swenson, Tom Tomas, Kristen Wendell, Jessica Watkins, Sara Willner-Giwerc, and Ziyi Zhang.

A huge thank you to everyone that has worked at Tufts CEEO past and present for all their dedication to pre-college engineering education.

Thanks to all the undergraduate students who have supported pre-college engineering education and especially Allison Kinzer and Marissa Zelten for their help with the artifact pictures for this book.

We want to express our deepest appreciation to Sherry Preiss for support with reading and editing, Emma Jones for photography support, Lynne Ramsey for graphic design, and Steven Andrews for cover design.

The authors wish to thank their partners (Chip, Vonda, Steven, and Dan) and children (Emma, Quinn, Jecha, Jerah, Jata, Asher, Lincoln, Austin, and Connor).

Portions of this material are based upon work supported by the National Science Foundation under grant nos. 2010139, 2010237, 1657218 1720334, 1316762, and 1020243. Any opinions, findings, and conclusions or recommendations expressed in this material are those of the authors and do not necessarily reflect the views of the National Science Foundation.

1

An Introduction to Engineering in K-8

Engineering can be an engaging and motivating experience for students of all ages. This book supports a wide range of educators: those curious about taking initial steps to include engineering in their curriculum, those who have been tinkering with engineering activities for a short while, and experienced educators who would like to enhance and fine tune their practice. This book is not intended to be a cookbook consisting of activities to be followed step-by-step. Rather, we encourage readers to leverage the ideas, activities, and examples to tailor their engineering in their classrooms in ways aligned to their interests and needs and those of their students.

Throughout this book, we offer glimpses of different classroom situations through case studies, examples, and pictures to illustrate the diversity of engineering approaches in many different settings that can meet the needs of *all* students. This includes developing or altering curricula to be representative of racially, ethnically, socioeconomically, neurodivergent, and gender-diverse populations. This book offers new engineering teachers a battery of tested activities to adapt to their own classrooms; in addition, we provide tools for educators to customize existing engineering curricula as well as develop their own. The classroom episodes and activity examples are taken from our partnerships with teachers as well as our own experiences in the classroom. As a note, we will use "teacher" and "student" throughout the book, but the approaches in this book are equally applicable to informal education settings.

Teaching engineering is about more than presenting students with a challenge and then handing them materials. It's also about being a responsive teacher who strives to understand students' ideas and supports them to enact

DOI: 10.4324/9781003378174-1

those ideas. With engineering experiences that are flexible and open-ended, students can gain an understanding of engineering, build agency and become confident, feel like they can make a difference in the world, and possibly see engineering as a career path.

Framing Vignette

We begin with a vignette of a group of fifth-grade students who designed a solution to a problem they identified in their classroom. The problem emerged while exploring a service-learning unit called "Community Inventions." After a series of design iterations, these students eventually created "The Guminator" to remove gum from classroom furniture.

To begin, the class watched a video of engineers solving problems. Then the students walked around the school identifying problems in the building. Next, they split into groups of four to discuss the problems identified in the walk-about, chose a problem for their group to tackle, and began brainstorming solutions. Part of their brainstorming involved thinking about their clients, their needs, and design constraints that could affect their designs.

One group picked the problem of gum that is stuck on the bottom of chairs and desks in their classroom. They felt it was a problem because the gum 1) is unsanitary; 2) hardens quickly on surfaces making removal difficulty; and 3) requires a call to the custodian for removal. Two students, Sasha and Sal, created their first prototype of their design: a plastic bag with two forks attached to it. See Figure 1.1. In their plan, the forks removed the gum, which then fell into the bag. They tested their design to see if it worked:

> *Sasha:* Is it working?
> *Sal:* Is it working? Yes, it works.
> *Sasha:* Now we just gotta make it so it falls into the bag easier.
> *Sal:* Yeah, I could, I could do that.

The forks pull the gum off the desk, but the way the bag is taped onto the forks and the lack of structure of the bag means that there is no space for the gum to fall into the bag. Sasha tells her group that it should be easier for the gum to get into the bag, implying that the user should not have to touch the gum. Here Sasha shows that she is thinking about the user as well as finding a solution to the problem. Keeping the user's hands off the gum becomes an explicit design criterion for the group and influenced their future designs.

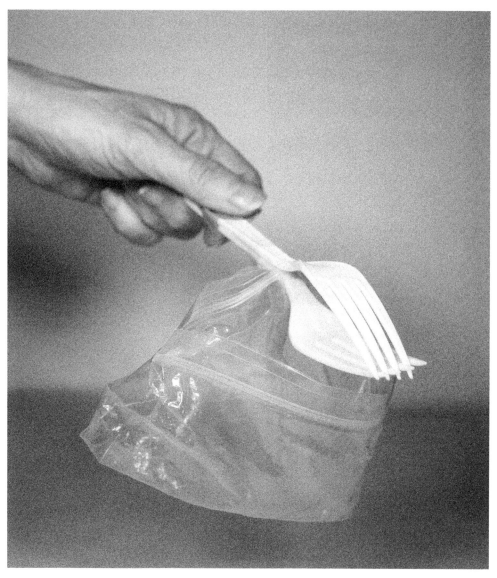

Figure 1.1 First iteration of the Guminator.

For the second version, the students use a plastic container covered with cardboard. The cardboard has a slot for the gum to fall through. They also change how the forks are attached and use a sleeve to cover and connect them so they can slide past each other (see Figure 1.2).

Upon testing, they find that the cardboard cover does not allow the forks to easily slide. Although the forks work as planned, the students substitute duct tape for the paper so the forks move more easily (see Figure 1.3). Again,

Figure 1.2 Second iteration of the Guminator.

this substitution of duct tape for paper shows that they are considering not only design function but also ease of use. They test this version, and the gum falls into the plastic container. After the group has tested their third iteration, a researcher walks up to the group.

> *Researcher:* So, are you going to . . . are you going to make any other models then since you have time next week?
>
> *Sasha:* Uuugghh.

Figure 1.3 Third iteration of the Guminator.

Researcher:	And then test them all against each other?
Sasha:	Actually, the first thing we did was a . . . ummm . . . we tried different liquids to get it to fall off.
Researcher:	Ahah.
Sasha:	That didn't work.
Researcher:	So.
Sasha:	Maybe if we coated the fork with a liquid, it would work better.

Based on this round of testing, the group identifies one part of their design they would like to improve—the ease of removing gum from surfaces. They decide to try a commercially available cleaner and find that it softens the gum, making it easier to remove. Their final design includes a holder for a bottle of liquid dissolvent and a scraper to remove the gum residue (see Figure 1.4).

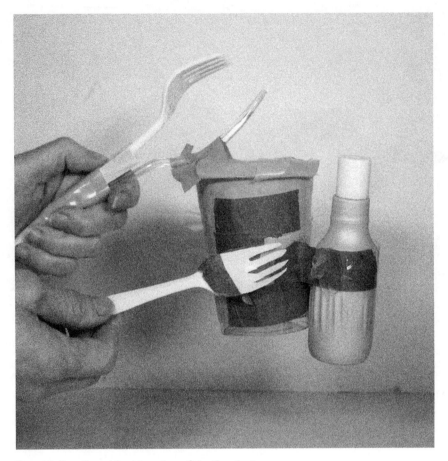

Figure 1.4 Fourth and final iteration of the Guminator.

Guminator Analysis

Throughout the Guminator's design process, the students engaged in several engineering design practices. They evaluated the usability and function of the Guminator through a series of tests. They looked critically at the data from the tests, pinpointing specific aspects that didn't meet their criteria, and redesigning to improve those features. To achieve authenticity and deeper understanding of the problem, the group used real gum. They researched aspects of their solutions such as which liquid would be the best to remove residue. Their teacher provided guidance and support, but they worked as a team to iterate on their original idea and end with a functional prototype.

Although this is just a short snippet from one of the classrooms with which we've worked, it shows students acting with agency throughout the entire engineering design process. The teacher presented the activity as part of a service-learning project; that is, students designed things to improve the school community. The open-endedness of the problem encouraged the students to choose problems that were personally relevant or meaningful to them. Students worked in small groups so that each student was able to contribute and physically work on the designs. Also, the students had enough time to do several design iterations, receive feedback from classmates, and then use the feedback to improve.

The planning and execution of the Guminator activity is grounded in our philosophy of engineering in the classroom, a pedagogical approach that fosters deep, inquiry-based learning and discovery.

Our Philosophy

Our philosophy of engineering in the classroom is built on a few basic tenets. First, we believe students are capable of engineering and have rich experiences and ideas on which to build. Second, we believe teachers are professionals who know their students the best and are most able to make decisions for the classroom while facilitating dynamic, classroom activities. Teachers can trust students to work through engineering challenges that are not overly structured and to deal with complex, messy problems.

Furthermore, we are committed to developing a citizenry with access to engineering thinking and experiences to draw upon as voters and across professions. Citizens who understand renewable resources, power systems, and clean air and water can participate in our democracy with greater thought and acumen. Understanding engineering concepts such as requirements, constraints, trade-offs, and iteration enhances their ability to analyze critical issues tied to political processes.

We also commit to teaching and learning that gives all students access to engineering learning and pathways. Historically, engineering has not been an inclusive profession, with significant communities excluded by curricular and systemic forces. Generally, engineering is largely dominated by white males, and engineering values and ideas have been centered around that population. Therefore, groups excluded based on race, ethnicity, socioeconomic status, gender identity, or the need for extra support due to neurodiversity are less likely to pursue the field of engineering.

Engineering for Young Students

Engineering in the classroom helps students work on a variety of skills. These include not only the Next Generation Science Standards for Engineering

Design but also standards and skills related to English, math, science, history, and social emotional learning. Engineering projects require more than standards proficiency or simply getting the correct answer. These projects engage students in authentic discourse as they work creatively and collaboratively to solve complex problems. Many students discover multiple solutions to the same problem. Teachers who leverage students' diverse experiences and ideas broaden access and enhance students' feeling of belonging. The overarching goal of the work is for students to feel good about what they are doing, feel competent about their work, and find engineering welcoming.

To make engineering more inclusive and welcoming, it's helpful for teachers to be intentional when presenting engineering to students. Building on students' assets rather than assessing their weaknesses and correcting misunderstandings promotes inclusivity. An asset-based approach honors past experiences, interests, and strengths.

Often engineering is perceived as being about race cars, rockets, and robots, which gives a message to students who are not interested in these things that engineering is not for them. Think back to the Guminator classroom: The students identified and then worked on problems that they found interesting. The trick is to recognize what students already know and provide scaffolds to help them grow; this will be a theme throughout this book. We advocate for children to have opportunities to engineer, but we acknowledge that what they do is different from what professional engineers do. Our role in facilitating their work is to find moments where they can engage in engineering behaviors and build skills, both engineering and otherwise, that they can use in the future.

Looking Forward

In the next chapter, we discuss engineering as a discipline and why engineering is suitable for children. Throughout the book, we present engineering activities students can do in the classroom. Often there will be an accompanying student vignette to illustrate what engineering looks like and to provide guidance in implementing engineering practices in the classroom.

This book is broken into three sections. **Section One** is an introduction to engineering, what it looks like for young students, and the hallmarks of hands-on, context-based engineering activities. **Section Two** brings the book's previous content to the practical aspects of the classroom. We present several case studies of varying lengths to help readers understand the classroom dynamics involved in engineering in the classroom and to help teachers anticipate what their own students may do. **Section Two** also includes several short engineering activities to implement, practice, and refine. **Section Three** talks about more complex engineering problems and practical logistics involved in planning and implementing engineering. We present several different activity contexts and discuss materials, assessment, documentation, and next steps in incorporating more complex design challenges. Teachers do not need to read this book straight through but can jump from chapter to chapter. We recommend that readers start with Chapters 1, 2, and 3 and at least two of the case studies. After that, it is possible to browse the sections of the book that meet specific classroom needs. We believe that this book can assist teachers in providing students with authentic engineering experiences requiring messiness, creativity, and agency. Numerous resources are also included in the appendix. We hope that readers will enjoy learning about the joy of introducing and practicing engineering with their students.

2

Engineering and Children's Powerful Designs

Second Graders as Engineers

Leticia and Maria, eight-year-old second-grade students, are working on designing a way to water plants in their classroom. They are doing engineering work. Their teacher, Anna, introduced the activity to the class by saying that they would be designing engineering solutions to some problems in the school. The class had already engaged in engineering activities in their classroom, but this was the most open-ended prompt they had received. Each pair of students is working on a different problem. Before each pair identified their problem, Anna led a whole-class discussion that helped the students think about problems in the school that could be solved using engineering. After this discussion, Leticia and Maria decide that they would like to figure out how they can make sure the classroom plants get watered over long breaks.

After researching and looking at different types of watering systems that already exist, they decide to try pipes or tubes to carry the water. They explore ideas about how water flows and how tubes and clamps can change the direction of the water. Leticia and Maria try several different solutions as they work. Some of their first ideas aren't successful; water only flows to the first plant. However, they analyze why their previous ideas were unsuccessful and redesign their solutions based on collected data. When they finally get a working prototype, they are elated.

There are many things to notice about Leticia and Maria as they engaged in the engineering activities. As Anna watched the pair, she saw them testing

DOI: 10.4324/9781003378174-2

their ideas at different times as they moved through the design process. Sometimes they tested the functionality of the entire design, but at other times, they tested out a small portion of the watering system to see where they could improve it. Anna was most struck by how they were learning to engineer as they worked through the engineering design process. As Anna walked around observing the students' work, she let each pair progress in the design process in ways that made sense for both the design and them. The students demonstrated a sense of agency and independence.

Beyond the science and engineering activities that Leticia and Maria did, Anna noticed that they collaborated, negotiated between competing design ideas, and clarified their scientific interpretations. She believed this engagement and agency was in part due to the way she, the teacher, had set up the engineering task; she had allowed students to build on their own ideas as they devised solutions for the problems. This open-endedness allowed students to approach engineering in a more equitable way since students drew on their own interests, strengths, and assets. Anna saw her work as the teacher as figuring out how to help students build on what they already knew and were excited about.

We have now presented two examples of how young students can engage in engineering, both in Chapter 1 and here in Chapter 2. Now, we will provide a brief history of engineering education and how it compares with how professionals engineer. This background information will enable you to see what engineering by adults looks like and to better understand the practices students are working toward.

> *How can young students develop engineering practices?*
>
> *How can engineering in the K-12 classroom support ALL students with a diverse range of backgrounds and experiences?*

From Professional Engineering to Engineering for Children

The inclusion of engineering in K-12 classrooms is a relatively recent development in US schools. Initial efforts to introduce engineering in K-12 classrooms were motivated by workforce issues—colleges and universities were not producing enough engineering graduates to fill the needs of corporations and government agencies. Higher education attributed the lack of engineering graduates to two facts: 1) high school students were not adequately prepared in math and science, and 2) high school students were unaware of the engineering profession and the many options it could afford. Emphasis was placed on students' value as potential engineers and lessening the shortage of engineers in the US rather than thinking about what students were getting out of taking engineering classes.

Transposing Professional Engineering to K-12

While the practice of professional engineering is central to the teaching and learning goals of K-12, it is not without its own tensions and challenges. Moreover, learning about engineering and engaging in engineering are two very different endeavors, especially when we consider the needs of children across K-12. In this section of this chapter, we describe how engineering has typically been defined and the ways in which elements of engineering are translated for K-12.

What Is Engineering?

We, the authors, define engineering as applying an understanding of the world in pursuit of solutions to problems. Engineers use what they know about the world to solve problems by creating a new thing or process, or by improving one that already exists. Engineering is often called "applied science" in reference to engineers drawing on knowledge in mathematics and science but then using that knowledge in service of developing a new solution to a problem. That is, engineers must be able to take technical knowledge and pair it with common sense and information gained from past experiences. They must also have a thorough understanding of a problem, as well as understanding both the end users and the stakeholders. Beneficiaries of engineering are not confined to humans, and users and stakeholders might think about how a design might impact animals or environmental considerations (Sanchez, 2023).

Who Are Engineers?

Often when people think of engineers, they envision someone sitting in front of a computer or working through a complex set of calculations with little connection to other people or the problem to be solved. While engineers sometimes work like this, most engineers focus on understanding the complexities of a problem and the end user involved with that problem. In addition, most engineers work on teams, collaborating frequently while solving these problems. Despite efforts to diversify the field of engineering, it continues to be a profession dominated by white males.

Thinking back to the classroom vignette at the beginning of this chapter, Leticia and Maria's teacher made engineering accessible to all the students in the classroom by letting them identify the problem they would solve.

Inadvertently, teachers constrain classroom engineering by requiring all students to solve the same problem, one that may or may not be personally relevant to the students, or by having all students follow the same path through the engineering design process.

Conversely, by allowing students to identify their own problem, as well as move flexibly through the engineering design process, teachers build students' confidence in creating diverse and relevant solutions, which are critical elements of engineering. This freedom to choose problems also aligns with the Next Generation Science Standards (National Research Council, 2013), which detail problem identification: "Engineers must be able to take the more technical knowledge and pair it with common sense and their past experiences." Young students can benefit from opportunities to build on their experiences and knowledge as they do engineering. This will in turn help them see that engineering can be a place for people from diverse backgrounds with varied experiences.

What Do Engineers Do?

Although there are numerous types of engineering (e.g., chemical, mechanical, materials), the overall goal of engineering is to solve problems. These problems may range from the grand engineering challenges like access to clean water to smaller issues such as creating a new nozzle for windshield wiper fluid. Often, engineers work in teams to create something new or improve something that already exists, or simply to help someone. Some team members do have direct contact with the intended end user they are helping, but usually engineers' contact with future end users is indirect.

The process that engineers follow is called the engineering design process (EDP). There are many different representations of this process, and although most of them make the process look very linear, engineers move back and forth between the steps as they work. Figure 2.1 is one representation of the EDP that we will use to anchor discussions throughout this book.

Drawings of the EDP are meant to be representations of the process used to ground discussions around the actions that form the process. Although the process is broken down into several specific actions, these actions are not meant to be a checklist. As we talk about each of these "steps," we will loop back to the example at the beginning of the chapter. Thinking back to Leticia and Maria's watering system, we can point to moments when they moved through the EDP. They identified the problem and then looked online to see what had already been done. They talked to their teacher to find out how much water the plants needed and how often they needed to be watered. They tried several different configurations of the tube system, making changes after each test they conducted.

ENGINEERING DESIGN PROCESS

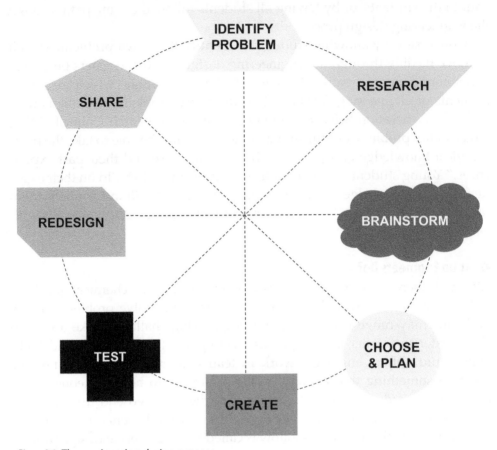

Figure 2.1 The engineering design process.

Remaking Engineering for Children

Engineers are individuals who use what they know about the world to solve problems by creating a new thing or process, or by improving one that already exists. Children, even as early as pre-kindergarten, have developed diverse ways of making sense of the natural world, ways of pursuing solutions to problems, and ways of communicating with others as they develop and apply knowledge. These diverse practices, or intellectual and linguistic resources, include children's use of language, gestures, ways of representing things and ideas, and varied perspectives on phenomena. Educators are encouraged to develop an asset-based stance toward the various contributions that children bring to engineering design activities. The asset-based approach posits that students have the capacity to have complex conversations about the world as they think about engineering problems and solutions. This approach to engineering instruction leverages the strengths and resources of all children.

Engineering activities for students focus on having students mimic engineering practices to gain engineering skills, but the activities are often decontextualized, with no links to real-life situations or contexts (Sanchez, 2023). Engineering with young students should include conversations and work that boost their understanding of the world and its interconnectedness. Working with children in this way helps them develop a more expansive world perspective beyond a sole focus on humans. While engineers do consider the needs and desires of humans who are involved, engineers should also think about how non-human entities are being impacted. For example, engineers might design a bridge to cut down on the distance commuters need to travel to cross a river, but this solution could negatively impact the communities and ecosystems on either end of the proposed bridge.

An asset-based approach includes Sanchez's (2023) point that as students are engineering, they should think about "What and who should scientists and engineers consider when developing technology and solutions?" Students have the capacity to have conversations that consider multiple, sometimes opposing views, and interact with the ethical aspects of design. Gunckel and Tolbert (2018) contend that social responsibility is part of engineering learning and that without its inclusion, we are not building students' capacity to empathize and consider multiple perspectives. Conversations during engineering time should also include examining the roles and responsibilities of engineers to their clients and the larger world.

Connecting With Students' Ideas and Building on Their Assets

Building upon students' assets and strengths requires educators to consider students' aspirations, contributions, and interests as they plan engineering experiences for their students. Practitioners must think expansively about what it means for students to engineer and how to connect to students' ideas.

Teachers must be able to make connections between students' interests and design activities that play to students' strengths and assets. What would it mean to consider students' interests by highlighting, acknowledging, and prioritizing engineering practices within these interests? Anna, the teacher in our example, built on Leticia and Maria's interest in keeping the classroom plants alive during long vacation breaks. In our own work, we have incorporated children's discussions and attention to fashion and considered ways in which engineering has impacted fashion industries through items such as sneaker design and technologies, wearable technologies, and breathable fabrics (e.g., Under Armor). Additionally, we have examined the ways in which engineering, with a focus on materiality, has impacted different sports like soccer, baseball, and basketball.

As we described in the previous section, connecting with children's interests requires an openness that positions children as potential contributors to the construction of engineering within K-12 settings. Practitioners should not make assumptions about students' interests or make stereotypical assumptions. Instead, they should make careful observations of children's practices and discussions.

Responding to Students' Ideas

These observations of students' practices and discussions help teachers support students to realize their ideas. We refer to this process of teachers connecting with students' ideas through eliciting, noticing, and responding to these ideas as *responsive teaching*. Responsive teaching is built on the principle that students' ideas and skill sets are worth including as a central part of teaching. The teacher's role during these engagements is to support the interactions and attend to them (Hammer et al., 2012). Throughout this book, we will come back to this idea of eliciting, noticing, and responding to students' ideas and how to facilitate engineering through supporting these ideas. Chapter 4 describes responsive teaching in more detail.

Coming Up: What Does Engineering for Children Look Like?

In the next chapter, we will talk about what engineering education looks like for K-12 students, with examples from a variety of classrooms. We will specifically highlight what it means to recognize and build upon children's assets and resources and explore what the EDP looks like with children.

References

Gunckel, K. L., & Tolbert, S. (2018). The imperative to move toward a dimension of care in engineering education. *Journal of Research in Science Teaching*, 55, 938–961.

Hammer, D., Goldberg, F., & Fargason, S. (2012). Responsive teaching and the beginnings of energy in a third grade classroom. *Review of Science, Mathematics, and ICT Education*, 6, 51–72.

National Research Council. (2013). *Next generation science standards: For states, by states*. Washington, DC: The National Academies Press.

Sanchez, A. (2023). Just worlding design principles: Children's' multispecies and radical care priorities in science and engineering education. *Cultural Studies of Science Education*, 18, 1041–1069. https://doi.org/10.1007/s11422-023-10197-w.

3

Children's Engineering

Knowledge, Skills, and Engagement

In this chapter, we'll look at four classrooms where teachers have presented design challenges. The first is a sixth-grade classroom that was part of a research project that explored student conversations and reasoning practices as they designed solutions to a real-world problem. We'll also introduce two third-grade classrooms, one in which students build bridges and another where they design an accessible playground. Finally, we'll present a second-grade classroom where the students build a water filtration system.

Turtle Egg Protectors

This initial example presents middle school students engaged in design conversations as they interpret and scope a real-world problem. Vera, their teacher, presented the problem of saving sea turtle eggs that were abandoned after a hurricane. Although the students constructed and tested devices to save the eggs, here we focus on the students' work prior to building these devices; Chapter 6 provides more information on the teacher's planning process and student outcomes. This vignette highlights student conversations regarding who should be allowed to be the turtles' caretaker using the devices the students designed. Vera facilitated impact talks in which students considered the ethical and moral impacts of their designs, not just the design building. As you read the following excerpt, pay attention to the structure that the teacher imposes for the classroom conversations regarding the design's impact.

DOI: 10.4324/9781003378174-3

On the first day of the activity, the teacher presented this problem: Design a safe way to transport the sea turtle eggs so that the eggs maintain a prescribed temperature range. The constraints included using a chemical reaction for the heating element, determining the size of the final device, and settling on the amount of time the students could spend on the project. Students were allowed to pick from a variety of construction materials to suit their designs.

On the second day of the project, Vera facilitated a problem-scoping discussion with the whole class. (See Chapter 10 for more information about facilitating classroom discussions.) As part of their problem scoping, the students brainstormed and debated additional criteria and constraints and named possible categories of users (scientist, average person, etc.). Vera used anchor charts to keep track of students' ideas and questions (see Figure 3.1).

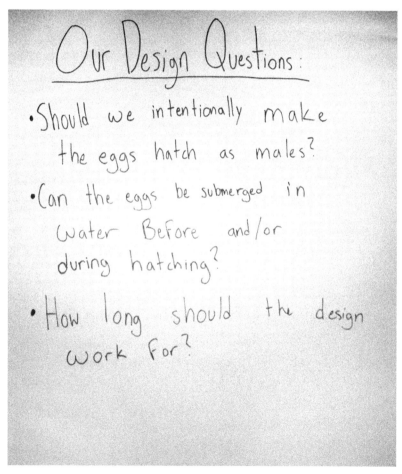

Figure 3.1 Anchor charts to record students' ideas about users and questions about the design.

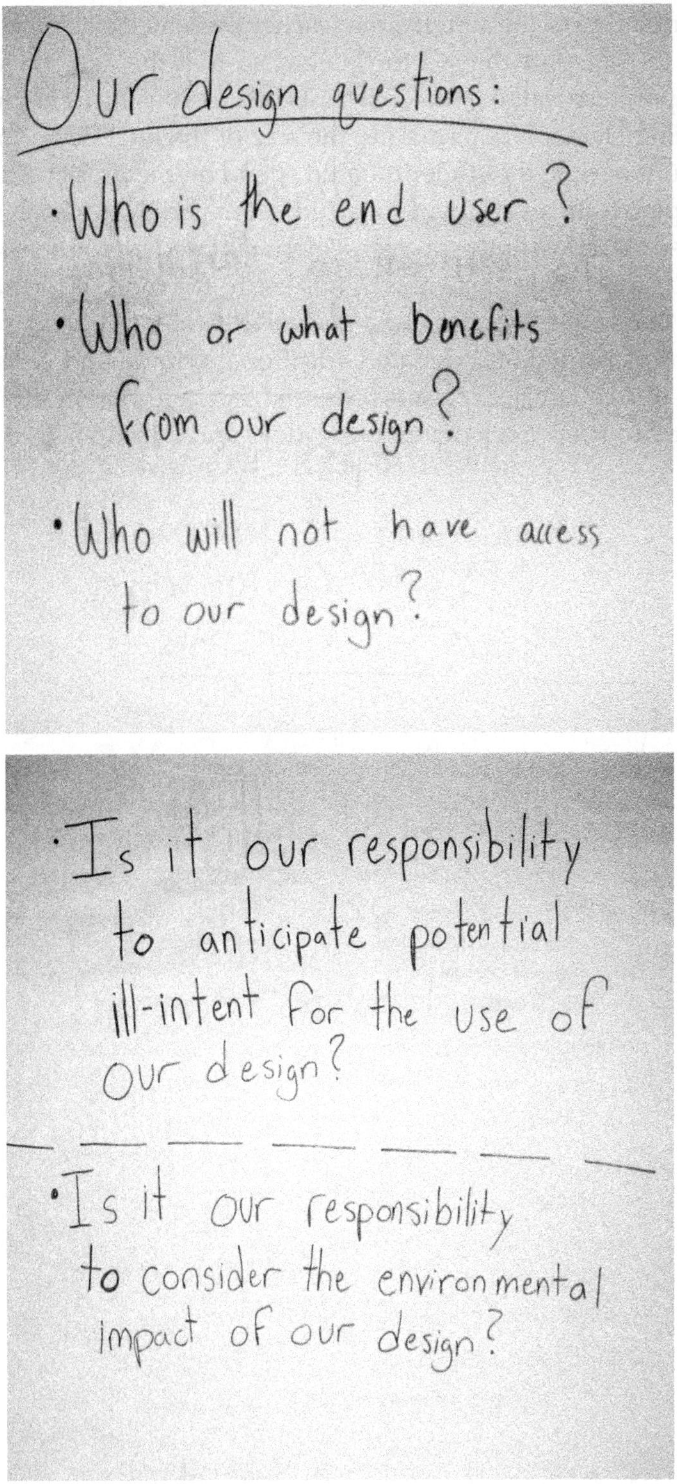

Our design questions:

- Who is the end user?

- Who or what benefits from our design?

- Who will not have access to our design?

- Is it our responsibility to anticipate potential ill-intent for the use of our design?

- Is it our responsibility to consider the environmental impact of our design?

Figure 3.1 (Continued)

Vera: Let's talk whole group; let me hear your thoughts. So in order for us to make this design something manageable and realistic, let's start considering who might potentially use our design. Should we just design for ourselves? Or should we kind of open it up to a bigger world? Yes Max?

Max: You could use it probably. We should probably open it up but um,

Vera: Yeah like who?

Max: Maybe some water associations that like try to help with turtles in specific, because our designs are meant for turtle eggs, aren't they?

Vera wrote Max's idea on the anchor chart.

Vera: So, like scientists who are already working—like trying—so that conservation center right? People who are actually trying to solve this problem. Yes, Nathaniel?

Nathaniel: Well, they're also, normal people just find them on the beach. We want it to be something that normal people can afford and use. So, it needs to be—it can't be extremely complicated.

Vera: Can't be extremely complicated, why not? Why can't it be extremely complicated? Yes, Nathaniel?

Nathaniel: Then they might not understand it, they might mess with it, and then they're breaking something.

Isabel: Then they could maybe um what is the word um ruin the temperature.

She continued to encourage students to consider possible users for the device, which prompted students' concerns about unintended consequences. The students began to link design outcomes to possible users. Thinking about potential users helped the students consider how much their device would benefit the turtles. They agreed that it was necessary to help the turtles, but they questioned who should use the device as not everyone might care for the turtles equally. For example, someone might get access to the eggs but decide to sell them rather than making sure that they could be safely moved.

JP: Maybe like someone really hates turtles and finds one and they like go up to a person on the beach, and they're like "I'm gonna save turtles but they hurt the eggs"

Vera: So, very interesting. So, let's go back to what JP said about potential, possibility, is it our responsibility to consider you know kind of ill intentions of random people?

As the students discussed who should be allowed to help the turtles, they considered the intentions, motivations, and background knowledge of different types of users. They imagined profiles for these different users and how each user might interact differently with the device. They felt that the average member of the public might threaten the turtle eggs but that people with a "scientific" background could hypothetically be better stewards of the eggs and more committed to saving them.

Student 1: I think if somebody finds the turtle eggs then they should call somebody who's like a professional, so they don't . . .

Student 2: Yes! Yes!

Vera: So, what are your concerns about regular people using the device?

Student 2: My concern is with anyone could buy it and if they wanted to do something bad with it, like take the eggs and sell them.

The students moved from talking about users to thinking about design criteria. See Table 3.1. Vera returns to an earlier comment from one student about the affordability of the device for some users.

Vera: So, I want to bring our conversation to money. So, you're saying because we already said that we want something [reading off board] affordable, easy to use, anyone can use and possibly even kids—does it have to cost money?

Student: Yes.

Table 3.1 Criteria and Constraints Named by Students and Transcribed by the Teacher Onto a Slide to Share in the Next Class

Criteria	Constraints
• Optimal temperature (29 °C) • Uses a chemical reaction as a heating element • Safe packaging of the egg (damage protection) • Safe to use • Simple design • Portable • Ventilated • Built with recycled materials ★ EXTRA: Easy egg pickup	• Size (must fit into a one-gallon Ziploc bag) • Time (two days in-class time to build) • Reaction materials: calcium chloride, water, baking soda

Vera: Why?

[lots of talking]

Student: Zero profit happens.

Vera: What do you mean?

Regina: If it doesn't cost money, then who would be paying to buy the parts? And then, after people give it out to people without getting any money back, you're just gonna end up broke.

Vera: Ah, ok. Yes Gabri?

Gabri: Yeah, yeah, I think it should cost money. Because like the people could use money for further research or like you can that money can help for a lot of things.

Vera: Interesting, I like that. So, Anthony what do you think

Anthony: I agree. You also think of what you do with the money. Incubator? There are so many things that need money that they could do with it. Clean up the ocean a bit.

Vera: Right so you could put the money to other uses. Nathaniel what do you think?

Nathaniel: Well, you could do is you could give them out to the beaches, the beach organizations, so that they're where they need to be, people can acc—people can get them if they find turtle eggs, and save the turtles, and then you don't have to give out as many either. People don't have to just buy them.

The students named additional constraints and criteria of the device: They again prioritized egg safety and purity as well as ease of use. To protect the turtles from unintended harm, they agreed to consult with scientists, experts in turtle migration.

Figure 3.2 highlights the EDP as we observed it during Vera's class discussion. During these conversations, the students engaged in problem scoping, researching and thinking about solutions, trade-offs, and optimization. Throughout their discussions, the students presented evidence of moving fluidly among the categories.

The context of the students' discussions went beyond the technical aspects of a design. Working together, the class reflected on the problem and arrived at constraints and criteria. Discussions included empathy and compassion alongside ethical considerations. During Vera's impact talk, the students talked about "who needs to have a voice in determining a solution, and what might be unintended consequences of a design." They thought about how to best advocate for the eggs. Engineering often addresses technology in terms of securing a human benefit while disregarding environmental or animal needs. Interested in preservation and safety, these middle school students demonstrated their environmental concerns.

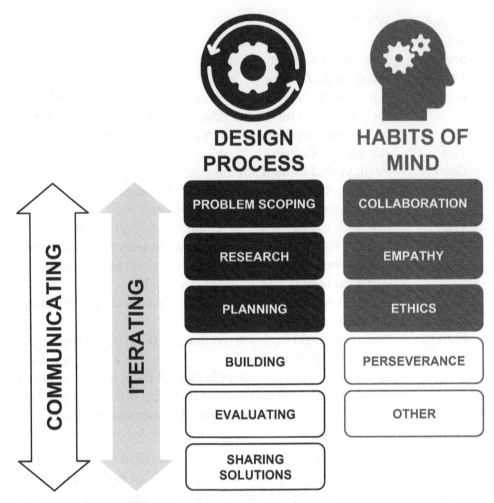

Figure 3.2 Engineering design practices during classroom discussion.

When students plan before they start building, they are doing much more than simply getting ready to build. We consider these planning conversations as real engineering and integral to the EDP. These types of discussions contribute to the students' construction of knowledge, inform their designs, and contribute to the development of the classroom community.

Asset-Based Approach

In the vignette, students used their knowledge of how the world works as they discussed this issue. Regardless of their building experience, their familiarity with the topic at hand, or their knowledge of engineering design, all students have assets and resources that can be useful for engineering. When Vera planned the unit, she thought about the knowledge students brought with them. She knew that they had differing levels of knowledge and experience with turtles as well as the understanding of the EDP. Yet *all students* could talk and think about the problem within an engineering context. We will address Vera's planning and thought process in greater detail in Chapter 6.

Throughout the class discussions, we could see evidence of engineering. When students engaged in problem scoping, they thought deeply about what to include in the design. The students put their clients, the turtle eggs, at the forefront of their decisions as they thought about design trade-offs. Teachers' willingness to look for and view students' resources as assets creates a space where students share their ideas and "show themselves." Remember that it's not necessary to do every "step" of the process every time. It's okay to focus on different portions of the process that will help students gain experience and learn.

Bridge Design

In this next example, third-grade students considered which craft materials to use as they planned a small-scale bridge with a twelve-inch span. They were new to engineering this year, and this was their second engineering activity. Their teacher, Jennifer, introduced the activity and led the class in a discussion about bridges. To each pair, she distributed a model with a river drawn on paper that was between two land masses represented by 6" cube boxes that they could use as they planned their bridges.

Jennifer emphasized planning in this activity and used student sketches as scaffolds to guide conversations within student groups. She stipulated that each group had to complete a drawing of their bridge and create a materials list. Jennifer provided a list of potential materials they could choose from and gave the students time to "play around" with various materials. Jennifer hoped that this exploration time would provide insight into the materials' properties. Walking around the classroom, she listened to their conversations and asked questions about their choice of materials.

> *Jennifer:* You listed string as one of your materials, but you don't have it on your drawing. Where would you use the string?

This conversation shows the planning process between CJ and Carrie as they try to figure out how to use string as part of their design:

> *Carrie* [grabbing the string and stated in a whispering tone]: What could we use this [piece of string] for?

CJ: Oh! Two strings because look you can hold this there and put tape right there and it will hold up the paper. Two pieces of string.

Carrie: Well then, we'll have to have . . .

CJ: Because this tape is strong.

Carrie: Okay. [pulls at the string in order to test its strength]

CJ: Okay, let's say here the paper [motioning to a space on the model]. We can put it under there and tape it like that. So, like the tape can hold the bridge if it tries to fall.

Carrie: Because the tape can hold it up.

CJ: I like it the way I did it. But if you like it the way you did it.
           Girl is writing on planning document.

CJ: Is that all?
           They both look at the document.

Carrie: We will need to cover our abutments. Oh, and we will need paper clips [grabs a paper clip].

CJ: Put the middle of the bridge

Carrie: [points to a few places on the platforms and counts out loud] *Three, four, five, six* [documents number of paper clips needed on their paper]

CJ: One, two, just two.
           Carrie is writing.

CJ: How many pieces of string?

Carrie: Do you think we'll need a popsicle stick?
           The girls pick up some popsicle sticks and discuss their list of materials.
           CJ counts something on the list then looks up with a huge smile.

Carrie: Do you think we could . . . could use this (popsicle stick)?

CJ: Oh, let me think about that.
           Students sit silently.

Carrie: Oh, we can use these to help hold up the . . . unintelligible.

CJ: That would be kind of difficult.

Carrie: So we'd . . . [motioning to the model]

CJ: I guess so.

Carrie: Done.
           They both raise their hands and look toward the teacher.

CJ: Okay, let's say here the paper [motioning to a space on the model]. We can put it under there and tape it like that. So, like the tape can hold the bridge if it tries to fall.

Carrie: Because the tape can hold it up. Do you think we could . . . could use this [popsicle stick]?

CJ: Oh, let me think about that.

Figure 3.3 illustrates the EDP skills observed in this vignette. Before the planning episode we described in this vignette, the two students scoped the problem and discussed potential solutions. During this planning conversation, the students thought about which materials to use considering their structural functionality. We saw evidence of informal testing when both students picked up materials and manipulated them to understand how the materials would work in their design: CJ demonstrated with tape and string, while Carrie picked up the popsicle sticks. The two students collaborated as they shared their ideas.

The EDP is a useful tool for planning, discussing, and reflecting on engineering design practices; however, as we discussed in Chapter 2, engineering, both in the classroom and for professional engineers, is messier than this model represents. As the students manipulated materials as part of planning, they evaluated their ideas and the appropriateness of materials; they thought about how to optimize their ideas and materials. Generally, when students are working on open-ended design projects, they move fluidly between engineering practices and behaviors, often engaging in more than one at a time.

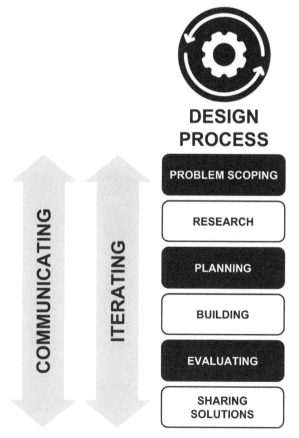

Figure 3.3 Engineering design skills visible during the bridge-building activity.

Open-ended projects that promote student agency, creativity, and collaboration are not always a neat process.

As you've seen in all the vignettes, there is not one predetermined pathway or solution that all students follow. Guided by the EDP, each student or group has unique conversations generating unique designs. In fact, there are even multiple representations of the process that serve as anchors supporting students as they engineer in the classroom. These visual representations usually present the EDP as a linear or cyclical process. In practice, however, the process is not linear or cyclical but more like a web, with frequent movement from one engineering behavior to another (Batrouny et al., 2021). Professional engineers also individualize their process based on particular projects. Both student and professional engineering teams sometimes benefit from an EDP visual representation as a useful engineering tool.

Playground Equipment

The next vignette presents third-grade students' use of the EDP as they design a piece of accessible playground equipment. Selena, Nina, and Lola spent four sessions designing, building, and iterating on their design. The researchers in the classroom kept track of their path through the design process to understand how they carried out their ideas to develop a "spinny thing" and build a prototype. See Figure 3.4.

Figure 3.4 Playground ride for students who use wheelchairs.

Selena, Nina, and Lola engaged in the activities of the design process but not in a linear, step-by-step path. The students moved flexibly, fluidly, and quickly between the different areas of the EDP (Batrouny et al., 2021). These young engineers rapidly iterated on their design ideas, moving between discussing an idea or building something and then evaluating that idea or product.

Student Agency: Engagement, Evolution, and Productivity

Students develop engineering skills and practices when they authentically engage in the design process. During the process, students are free to make their own choices as they have discussions, choose materials, and change design direction. Student agency helps students practice and develop their skills as they experiment, make mistakes, get feedback, and learn from these mistakes. In addition, students' engineering practices evolve with time and experience, allowing them to more easily anticipate or observe how their design ideas will play out. Through engineering, students' ideas can deepen their understanding of how the world works.

Engineering is a creative process characterized by bursts of progress as well as periods that are less obviously productive. Sometimes students focus and move quickly, and other times, they may be off track or stuck. Although students may appear unproductive, they are simply working through ideas. Conversations with their classmates as well as their teachers help students reflect on their progress and manage frustration.

As students are working, the teacher acts as a facilitator. While guiding the egg protector discussion, Vera helped students make sense of their ideas but did not intervene to correct them or present her own ideas as conical knowledge. We will talk more about the role of the teacher and supporting students in Chapter 4.

Social Dynamics

Just like any group endeavor, it's hard to balance different ideas and work-flows in engineering design. Teachers can support productive collaboration using classroom structures and practices. Collaborating in pairs or small groups can be especially difficult when students are beginning to engineer since they are now working with new social expectations and navigating new social dynamics. Learning to negotiate, manage disagreements, and compromise are integral parts of collaborative teamwork and essential to the design process.

Water Filtration

Let's look at a group of second-grade students who are designing a water filter. The teacher had already introduced the activity and the engineering design process and provided each group with a box of materials: mesh screen, coffee filters, plastic cups, a two-liter water bottle, sand, and gravel. Each student had a planning worksheet that included a space for them to draw their design. Danny, Trenton, and Elijah knew they needed to build one filter between them but had different ideas of what this should look like. When discussing the plan, the challenges of group collaboration emerged as the boys worked toward envisioning their design. The boys had to decide which materials to use and how to hold them together. Two of the boys focused on using the sand and gravel, while the third boy thought about using the screen and coffee filters as part of the filter.

Danny: Sand [tapping on the cup of sand], water [tapping on the cup of water], and this to go in this [screen to go in the two-liter bottle].

Trenton: Wait, the screen? Yeah, we can't put the screen [here], it's too little [top of the bottle].

Danny: You can put this right in [placing the coffee filter in a plastic cup].
   Elijah and Trenton say "No, no."

Elijah: We're making . . . about talking, mixing things together.

Trenton: We're talking to draw a picture.

Danny: Oh, this [screen] will fit in there [bottle]. I know how. Turn it over and put this in there [grabbing the coffee filter].

Trenton: Danny, you don't know what you are doing.
   Elijah takes bottle turns it over and places the coffee filters in the bottom, which has been cut off, so the bottle is open on the bottom.

Danny: See if you push it in there.
   It worked, but Elijah and Trenton denied that it would stay. Danny grabbed the bottle and put the filter inside to show them that if you pushed it down a little it would stay in place.

Trenton: Danny, no, you can't do that.
   Danny put everything back in the box with the rest of the materials.

The students sat silently for a few seconds, seemingly unsure of what to do next. Elijah and Trenton began talking about combining the sand and gravel. Danny's head was down. Elijah and Trenton continued to talk to each other. Danny looked up and then picked up his pencil and the planning sheet.

Trenton: You can't use this [coffee filter]. It will rip.
        Danny pointed to something in another part of the room—another group using a coffee filter. I used that before. See it won't rip on this.
Elijah: They just don't know. They just don't know it will rip.
        Trenton said that he used a water filter with another group, and it did not rip. It just went through it. Danny asked a student in another group who was next to him if it ripped when they used it.
Danny: It did not rip. Haha. I win.
Trenton: Nu-uh. We have to vote.
Danny: Then go over there and see (pointing to the group that is successfully using a coffee filter).
Trenton: Let's vote.
Danny: You're just going to pick his. Aren't you?
        The teacher joined the group.

Although the three students grappled with their ideas collaboratively, they didn't know how to agree on next steps. There are a few ways to support students to come to a consensus: 1) Students could do mini tests of different ideas; 2) before, during, and sometimes after the lesson, the teacher might discuss with the students ways to reach consensus and have productive conversations; 3) teachers could lead a brainstorming activity to explore different ideas.

Benefits of Including Engineering in K-8 Classrooms

How does engineering in the classroom benefit students? Students gain skills beyond the ability to construct devices. There is a wide range of knowledge, skills, and attitudes that students gain while engaging in engineering. As seen in the water filter vignette, sound engineering practices include collaboration, negotiation, and consensus building. Students also build conceptual knowledge of engineering and related disciplines. In addition, they improve their executive functioning and social-emotional competence. Finally, they gain an appreciation for how engineering can impact the world and the significant role they can play in advancing this impact.

The primary goal of doing engineering design with young children is *not* about trying to turn all students into engineers. It is to show students that engineering is for *everyone* and to give them the chance to try out engineering. Students may not choose to become professional engineers, but engineering can influence how they see the world. As they get older, they can use this knowledge to understand how things were designed and the conversations that design teams may have had as they create objects. An understanding of engineering benefits decision making, especially when social, ethical, and environmental concerns surface in development and implementation.

For example, trusting driverless cars goes beyond understanding how they work mechanically; it is valuable to understand the algorithm that engineers used when deciding how driverless cars interact when choosing between hitting another car or striking a person. When engineers grapple with a design issue, they consider a panoply of design implications. For example with driverless cars, their work cannot be limited to mechanical issues; they must consider the environmental impact as well. Additionally, the ways a problem is presented lead to different conversations and levels of civic understanding and engagement.

Finally, engineering is a discipline that offers all students of varying talents, abilities, backgrounds, and skills an opportunity to be creative problem solvers and builders. Including engineering in classroom curricula helps all students feel capable of engineering, with some students envisioning engineering as a possible future career. Research provides evidence that there is a connection between students' engineering role identity and their motivation to pursue engineering as a career (Godwin, 2020). Godwin (2020) provides further reasons for students to engage in authentic engineering tasks. Students build competence in a wide array of skills and receive recognition for that competence. Engineering is not only for students who are part of a gifted and talented program. All students have talent, experiences, and skills that they can apply to a wide array of engineering activities, adding diverse and unique perspectives.

References

Batrouny, N., Wendell, K., Andrews, C., & Dalvi, T. (2021). Mapping students' engineering processes with design zones. *Science and Children*, 58(3), 61–65.

Godwin, A. (2020). Identity-based motivation: Connections between first-year students' engineering role identities and future-time perspectives. *Journal of Engineering Education*, 109(3), 362–383.

4

The Responsive Engineering Classroom

Classroom Culture: Establishing Norms, Expectations, and a Community of Collaboration

Classroom norms foster collaboration and engagement and provide students with clear guidelines. Norms also nurture diversity of actions, ideas, skills, and backgrounds when they are designed to be inclusive. Setting clear guidelines supports students to act as engineers as they take risks, act independently, and demonstrate flexibility. We encourage explicitly addressing norms and expectations as part of the introduction to engineering. Including students in the process of establishing classroom norms enhances student investment in these norms. Many teachers also find that the norms introduced as part of engineering provide fruitful structures for work in other disciplines.

Engineering requires a high level of collaboration and sharing, both with project partners and during whole class discussions. Although **listen to each other** is a common classroom norm, it is often applied only to listening to another student when they are presenting something. We apply this norm to *always* listening to each other. In fact, many teachers reinforce this norm when students brainstorm ideas or iterate on their designs. Another norm that encourages creativity is **wild ideas are okay**. Inviting wild ideas helps students feel comfortable sharing their ideas, even if they think they might not be worthy of consideration. A third norm that promotes collaboration is **there are no private ideas**. This norm counters students' feeling that someone has "copied" or "stolen" their idea. Competition is a classroom structure that can work against collaboration; students may feel that their success is based

DOI: 10.4324/9781003378174-4

on other students not doing as well as they are or having ideas that are less worthy. Another norm aimed at collaboration is **be respectful when critiquing and move forward together**.

If teachers discuss these norms with students before they start working, students might be more inclined to build on each other's ideas as a group rather than individually. It may also be helpful to have a lesson on respect since students are often hesitant to critique each other's ideas. Often students will try to combine ideas to be respectful of each other; they see blending ideas as a compromise without realizing that blending may not lead to the best outcome or a workable design. Instructors can talk about what it means to identify something negative in someone else's design and that the purpose of the critique is to help groups have the best design possible.

When engineering, students are practicing these new norms and expectations, which may counter the more common school norms. Typically, students are used to working toward the "correct" answer or following explicit instructions. For example, with most math assignments, students are required to arrive at the same answer with little room for alternate solutions. When engineering, we often see students asking teachers if they are doing the "right thing" or what they should do next. Therefore, when teachers introduce engineering activities, they might remind students of one basic norm, that is, their ideas are front and center and when engineering, there is no right answer. As facilitators, teachers can help students learn to take risks, share and assess their own ideas, and learn from peer feedback in addition to the teacher's.

These norms and expectations, which foster a community of collaboration, will not only help students work together but will shift the dynamic from pleasing the teacher to considering others' ideas and giving feedback to each other. At first, teachers may need to scaffold ways to collaborate by reinforcing norms and expectations as students engage in the design process. However, in time, students will not only reflect on their own ideas but give each other useful feedback to support the design process.

Facilitating Engineering

While teaching engineering, there are multiple things happening at one time, and teachers must make numerous in-the-moment decisions based on what students are doing and saying. Teachers' decisions and actions are most productive when they create a classroom where students ideas are valued and they provide equitable opportunities for students to engage in engineering (Miel et al., 2023).

While students are working, teachers act as facilitators who notice and respond to students' ideas as they brainstorm, design, iterate, build, and move through the engineering design process. We want to foster student agency and give students the freedom to creatively solve problems. This means that they will pull from their own resources rather than relying on the teacher to lay everything out for them. It also means that not all students are doing the same thing; even within groups, students may take on different roles. There are different ways for students to contribute. It is not only the student who builds who is the engineer. Equal attention should be paid to the different roles.

Characteristics of Student Agency in a K-8 Engineering Classroom

★ Students feel confident in using their own ideas and voices throughout the engineering design process.
★ Students are motivated by following their ideas rather than trying to figure out what the teacher wants them to do.
★ Students are not solving problems in the same way or following the EDP at the same pace.
★ Students are not asking the teacher what they should be doing but asking their teammates.

Responsive Engineering Teaching

We briefly mentioned it in Chapter 2, but we will delve deeper into responsive engineering teaching in this chapter. Responsive teaching is a model of teaching in which students' ideas are at the forefront of interactions as educators recognize and support students' ideas (van Es & Sherin, 2008, 2021; Robertson et al., 2016). Teachers select instructional moves in the moment in response to students' ideas. Responsive teaching is not specific to engineering; it is used in all disciplines with students from kindergarten through college. Responsive teaching includes instructional moves in which teachers elicit, notice, interpret, and respond to students' work and conversations. A brief overview of each of these instructional moves follows.

Eliciting

Teachers elicit their students' thinking by presenting questions or tasks to engage students in a conversation or activity and invite them to share ideas. Open-ended design activities allow for multiple ideas and interpretations, strengthening creativity and student agency. Rather than looking for a specific or single answer, the teacher focuses on the students' ideas. Recall the vignette with Vera's class and the turtle eggs. In that situation, Vera elicited the students' ideas with a simple prompt: "What do you mean?" At another point in the conversation, students shared concerns about "regular" people using the device. Vera simply probed, "What are your concerns about regular people using the device?" In both cases, Vera's prompts stemmed from the students' ideas without introducing any of her own ideas about the turtle protectors.

Noticing and Interpreting

Noticing involves focusing on students' work and discourse and then making sense of it. Observing and interpreting provide teachers with insight into their students' thinking and their past experiences. Teachers often do not consider students' work as engineering because it doesn't resemble the work of professional engineers. However, the work students do when they first start engineering should be considered productive beginnings of engineering. For example, when two students talk about a design, their discussion may not mimic exactly that of a professional engineer. However, they are demonstrating behaviors they will build on as they develop engineering practices. Teachers noticing what students are doing also aligns well with an asset-based approach.

Responding

Responding means that using the in-the-moment information teachers notice and interpret, they adjust their lessons quickly and flexibly to meet students' needs (see Table 4.1). With this approach, teachers respond with follow-up questions, new directions, or focused discussions. We saw Vera pivot quickly based on the ideas students brought to the whole-group discussion. Although she had considered the initial discussion about the turtle protectors, she had not expected her students to spend so much time discussing who should use the devices. Vera responded by creating space for her students to expand their ideas about who would be responsible users.

Why Do We Like Responsive Teaching for Engineering?

Responsive teaching practices pair well with open-ended engineering design activities. Engineering calls for creative and diverse ideas, and responsive teaching supports a classroom where students find multiple entry points into conversations and designs. A responsive approach fosters equitable consideration of all students' ideas and experiences. All students receive the opportunity to participate, experience success, and feel a sense of belonging.

Table 4.1 Responsive Teaching Phases

	Elicit	**Interpret/Notice**	**Respond**
What the teacher does	Present a task with multiple ways to do it and multiple solutions.	Understand what students are saying and thinking.	Make instructional choices and revisions based on noticing and interpreting students' ideas.
Purpose	Provide ways for students to connect their own interests, ideas, and assets with the task. Include all students' ideas and voices.	Identify early engineering ideas and practices. Make sense of students' ideas.	Respond to students' specific ideas. Help students interpret their own ideas. Help students figure out next steps to build on ideas.

Responsive teaching is one way to make sure students' ideas are at the center of their engineering work. While students discuss their design ideas, teachers can employ specific strategies or teacher moves that further promote and refine the students' ideas. Based on work by Miel et al. (2023), these engineering teacher moves are categorized as ambitious, conservative, and inclusive. Ambitious teacher moves "encourage student reasoning about a design problem or solution" and include asking open-ended or probing questions, making open-ended statements, or pressing students for answers. Conservative teacher moves include eliciting a specific type of answer, requesting a simple fact, evaluating correctness, and helping students manage the design process. These moves help teachers assess student understanding of a concept or remind students of the task and remaining time. Inclusive teacher moves aim to give all students the opportunity to have a voice in discussions, design processes, and products. Inclusive strategies include acknowledging students' contributions and create discussion norms that ensure all students participate.

How Does Responsive Teaching Enable Engineering in the Classroom?

Engineering solutions don't have one "correct" answer; similarly, there is not one correct way to teach. We're going to share a few classroom scenarios to show what engineering education can look like. The first example illustrates a highly structured fourth-grade lesson in which the instructor provides students with all the answers. The introductory engineering unit focuses on the concept of buoyancy. The students are building a boat that needs to hold five pennies. Each student has a piece of aluminum foil and five pennies.

Teacher: To see how buoyancy works, we are going to build boats that will hold five pennies. Fold up the sides of the tin foil so that it will hold the pennies without sinking. Let's take ten minutes to make your boats, and then we'll all bring them the sink so we can test them.

As the students worked, the teacher walked around the room, giving them suggestions about how to fold the aluminum foil. At one point, she told them to make sure that they seal all the edges when they fold the sides so water does not seep in. After ten minutes, she told the students to bring their boats to the sink. Each group placed their boat in the sink to test it, and the teacher placed the pennies one at a time on the boats.

Teacher: Great job, Annie and Jose, your boat was able to hold all five pennies. Why do you think it could float?

Annie and Jose looked at each other, unsure of what to say.

Teacher: It starts with a "b."

Annie: Boy . . .

Teacher: That's right, buoyancy. Next, Hoda and Marco, try yours.

Hoda and Marco put their boat in the water. It began to sink after three pennies.

Teacher: Your boat started to sink. Look at this corner and see how you did not seal the edges, so the water was able to sneak in and make the boat sink. If you have more time, you should pinch the foil together to seal the hole. Good job!

The teacher moved on to the next group.

In that set of exchanges, there was little evidence of the elicit–notice–interpret–respond paradigm of responsive teaching. In addition, the task was not open or robust enough for students to engage and have conversations around it. Finally, the teacher gave basic instructions and then walked around the room making sure the students all followed the instructions exactly.

The teacher asked the students to share why they thought their boat was floating. However, she then cut off Annie when she was partially through the word that the teacher was looking for. In this instance, the teacher was interested in all students knowing the word buoyancy but didn't give the students time to explain what they thought buoyancy is and how it's connected to their project. In that moment, the teacher missed an opportunity to note, interpret, and build off the students' ideas. When Hoda and Marco tested their boat and it sank, the teacher analyzed Hoda and Marco's boat and then told them how to fix it. The moment their boat began to sink could have been a moment to listen to and understand the students' thinking, as in this exchange that exemplifies a responsive teaching approach:

Teacher:	Your boat just started to sink. Why do you think that happened?
Marco:	I'm not sure.
Teacher:	Marco and Hoda, look at your boat in the water. Why do you think it is happening?
Hoda:	Oh, look! Water is going into the boat in that corner!
Marco:	Oh, yeah. We should have sealed it better. Can we fix it?
Hoda:	Can we fix it and test it again?
Teacher:	Sure! What do you think you can do to seal it better?
Hoda:	I think we can bend that piece of foil (pointing) around that part so they meet and there's not a hole.
Teacher:	I'm interested to see what happens when you do that. You can make changes after everyone tests their boats.

In this exchange, the teacher facilitated the conversation rather than directly telling the students what to do. She posed open-ended questions with the purpose of narrowing their focus to think about specific things, such as "Why do you think this is happening?" This open-ended question made the students' thinking visible. She also used the same language as the students—"What do you think you can do to seal it better?"—so that her words would not be misinterpreted by the students as directions or communicate that she was looking for a specific answer. As indicated, responsive teaching encourages the teacher to play the role of facilitator and allows for students' ideas to take priority. The responsive teaching scenario of this activity unfolded in this way. First, the teacher set up the task to make boats to introduce the concept of buoyancy. She assigned the task of making boats to hold pennies and showed the students a table of materials. She told them to make a quick sketch of their boat, label it, gather the materials to use, and then start to build. Before the students began to work, the teacher asked the students if any of them had ever been on a boat before. Some of the students raised their hands. The teacher also showed the students a few pictures of boats.

Teacher:	Let's look at a few pictures of boats. You can see that some boats are really big, and some are only big enough for. . . . Can someone tell me what they notice about these pictures of the boats?
Student 1:	They have some place people can sit.
Student 2:	The front is pointy, and the back is flat.
Student 3:	Some of the boats have sails.
Teacher:	What do you notice about what they are made of?

Students suggested materials such as wood, metal, and plastic. The conversation continued a bit longer, and then the teacher told them to begin building their boat according to any design they wished provided the boat could float and hold pennies. She encouraged them to test their builds in the testing station as they progressed.

The teacher structured this activity as an open-ended task to elicit student thinking. For example, the students used their own ideas about what to design and were able to draw from their own varied past experiences with boats as well as materials. Since students' experiences with materials varied, the teacher was not looking for one specific design. In fact, by welcoming a variety of designs and ideas, the teacher built upon the students' existing resources and experiences.

Pairs of students began to talk about which materials would help the boat float and sketch out their plans. As they worked, the teacher walked around the room checking in with each group, asking them questions about the boats they are designing. She stopped beside Josh and Tia who were deep in conversation.

Teacher:	Which materials are you planning on using?
Tia:	We were thinking we would use cardboard, duct tape, and popsicle sticks.
Teacher:	Can I see your drawing so I can see how you will use them?
	Tia moves back so the teacher can see their drawing.
Teacher:	Can you explain this part here?
Josh:	This is the part in the water.
Teacher:	The popsicle sticks?
Josh:	Yes. We'll put paper on top of the popsicle sticks and use the tape to attach them.
Tia:	We thought the tape would make it waterproof too!
Teacher:	Oh, so the tape is really doing two things: keeping the popsicle sticks together and making the bottom of the boat waterproof.
Josh and Tia:	Yes!
Teacher:	Do you think the water will come over the sides?
Tia:	We were thinking that, but Josh said he was on a raft, and the raft didn't have sides.
Teacher:	That makes sense. So you are making a raft rather than a boat.
Josh:	Yes, is that okay?
Teacher:	Sure, as long as it can float and hold pennies.
Josh:	Can we get materials now?
Teacher:	Sure, don't forget to test your raft before we all share.
Tia:	Okay.

In this exchange, the teacher tried to understand the students' design and why they made certain choices. She asked questions intended to push their thinking, specifically about the water coming over the edges. The teacher had a much different type of floating device in mind but was satisfied with the students' thinking creatively about the task and using their ideas instead of hers.

The teacher left that group and continued to talk to groups around the room. Pairs of students tested their builds as they worked. The teacher allowed them to work at different paces. Some students had built their boats and wanted to see if they could hold pennies. Other groups tested parts of their boats to see if they were waterproof. She walked over to one group who had been at the testing station for a few minutes, and they were very animated.

> *Teacher:* What are you testing?
> *Kamala:* We made our boat, but it won't float.
> *Ajay:* It starts to go underwater. We keep adding things to make it float, but it won't work.
> *Teacher:* That must be frustrating. Can you show me?
> *Ayay:* It is.

Ajay put their boat in the water. It sat on the top of the water for a second and then started to slip under.

> *Ajay:* See! We keep trying and it's still not working.

Ajay and Kamala started putting packing peanuts on top. The boat continued to slowly go underwater. They kept adding the packing peanuts.

> *Kamala:* It doesn't matter how many we add, it keeps sinking.
> *Teacher:* This seems really frustrating. So you are adding the peanuts trying to make it float?
> *Kamala:* Right, but it doesn't matter.

The teacher was confused by what the students were doing, so she continued to ask questions.

> *Teacher:* Did you always plan to add the packing peanuts or just when your boat started to sink?
> *Ajay:* It wouldn't float so we thought adding them would make it better.
> *Teacher:* So, you added the peanuts hoping that the boat would float? Why?

Ajay:	It would help it float because peanuts are so light and float.
Teacher:	So, adding the peanuts will help because the peanuts float and they will help the boat float. Do you think there's a certain amount you need?
Kamala:	We weren't sure, so we kept adding them.
Teacher:	If I added peanuts to something that usually sinks, would it make that item float. What do you think it is about the packing peanuts that will make things float.
Ajay:	Probably. If you add enough. I think that the peanuts float really well because they are so buo . . .
Teacher:	Buoyant?
Ajay:	Yes.
Teacher:	Hmm. This is an interesting idea. Maybe we should think about this as a class.

In this exchange, the teacher noticed Kamala and Ajay's ideas about the packing peanuts and asked questions to understand their thinking. Though the teacher was pretty sure that the students thought that adding the packing peanuts on top of the raft would somehow make the raft float, she asked questions to understand how this idea shaped their design choices. Additionally, she encouraged them to pursue their ideas rather than correcting them.

The teacher circulated around the classroom asking students if they thought their materials would help their boats float. She was surprised by their assumptions about buoyant materials and the concept of buoyancy. She realized that that this lack of understanding affected their ability to do the activity. Therefore, the next day during science time, she decided to do a hands-on activity about floating to help students discern which materials float and which do not so that they could return to the previous engineering activity with the boats. She assumed that hands-on testing of the materials' buoyancy would more effectively support their conceptual understanding than an explanation.

The next day, she had the students go through a variety of materials and predict which would float. To record the data, she put an anchor chart on the wall with two columns: floats and does not float. One by one, students chose an item, made a prediction as a whole class, and then put the item in the water to see if it would float or sink. She was surprised, again, that so many students had predicted that putting packing peanuts on top of something would help it float. After the class had tested all the items, they looked at the columns and discussed the properties of the different materials. The class then discussed the materials on the "float" column in terms of the boats they were building. The next day, the class finished working on the boats, referencing the anchor chart. With this expanded knowledge of the materials, the students were better able to complete the boat activity.

Teacher as Facilitator

A responsive engineering classroom will often include open-ended engineering activities designed to foster creativity and solution diversity. A responsive classroom may look messy, with different groups of students designing different things as the students engage authentically in the problem-solving process. Individuals and groups of students approach the EDP in their own unique ways. Therefore, students thrive and engage with this process when teachers practice responsive teaching, acting as facilitators to guide and support students rather than simply delivering answers.

With the group using packing peanuts, the teacher asked questions followed by a stand-alone activity to help the students discover and solidify the concept of buoyancy rather than simply telling the students that peanuts do not make things float. Teachers can also support students through probing questions and thoughtful conversations that can encourage them to think more deeply or differently. Research shows that certain teacher questions prompt student reasoning within engineering (Capobianco et al., 2018). Promoting reasoning and expanding student thinking through questioning can happen anytime—during whole class discussions, checkins within group work, or any activity.

Managing Student Frustration During the Engineering Design Process

Engineering design is an iterative process that often involves failed attempts. When students are having difficulty or seem frustrated, it's okay to empathize with them. Recalling Ajay and Kamala, the teacher sensed their frustration over their boat not floating. Instead of cheerleading, affirming their design, or telling them to think more, the teacher empathized with them and said, "That must be frustrating." This empathetic statement named and acknowledged their frustration. During the EDP, some students' designs are not going to work, and students will become frustrated. Sometimes, the frustration is small, and students will quickly move past it. Or sometimes, students will need to take a break for a few minutes. Teachers can help students learn from these moments of failure and frustration by providing coping mechanisms such as breaks or conversations to reframe failure as a positive component of engineering. Remind students that even professional engineers cope with failure often and that sustained effort is part of engineering.

However, sometimes students are so frustrated that they are unable to move forward in the process. They are simply stuck. At this point, one strategy is to problem solve or co-design with them. For example, teachers could offer students several design choices and discuss them together. Or, if students are highly challenged by trying to physically build something, it may be appropriate for teachers to help them out with their own hands. The solution may be as easy as the teacher helping students glue two things together.

In this next scenario, a pair of sixth-grade students tried to build a device that uses a wheel and axle. The teacher noticed that they had been working on the same part of the design for almost thirty minutes. He checked in a few times and gave support, but they weren't making progress. The teacher feared that if they continued to focus on the wheels and axles, they wouldn't have enough time to work on the cart they had planned.

Teacher:	How is everything going? What are you working on?
Kyle:	Fine. We are trying to make this wheel work.
Teacher:	Can you show me how you want it to work?
Kyle:	We want it to work like this (showing the pieces they are using), but the middle part of the wheel won't work.
Teacher:	What have you tried?
Genna:	We've tried everything, and the middle keeps slipping out, especially when we try to move it. We're never going to have time to make it and do the rest of our thing.
Teacher:	I have an idea if you want to try it. I really want you to have enough time to finish your cart, but it looks like this axle is going to take a while. I have a wheel and axle from a kit. Would you like to use those? You have a lot of great ideas for your cart, and I think this means you'll have more time to make those happen.
	Kyle and Genna look at each other and appear to be uncertain.
Teacher:	It's up to you, but even professional engineers work in big teams and do not make everything themselves. They look at what materials they have already and think about using them.
	Kyle and Genna look at each other again and nod their heads.
Genna:	Sure, we can try that.

Teachers have to determine the right kind of support at the right time. If students are so frustrated they are not able to participate, an intervention might be necessary. Using prebuilt pieces for smaller parts of a design can reduce frustration and allow students to prioritize work on the larger parts.

Engineering learning in K-8 classrooms is a time for students to be creative and build on their own ideas. By creating shared norms and practicing responsive teaching, teachers can act as facilitators who understand their students' ideas and support them as they engineer creative solutions to relevant problems. As students follow different timelines during the EDP and possess different ideas, this time can be chaotic. At first, this chaos and lack of uniformity might challenge both students and teachers, but over time together, they'll build a classroom culture of mutual listening and support. The next section of this book is going to define and explore productive engineering activities and highlight the practical aspects of the classroom through case studies. Chapter 5 will present the principles of "good" design activities and offer concrete, classroom-based examples of activities including strategies for student engagement.

References

Capobianco, B. M., DeLisi, J., & Radloff, J. (2018). Characterizing elementary teachers' enactment of high-leverage practices through engineering design-based science instruction. *Science Education*, 102(2), 342–376.

Miel, K., Swanson, R. D., Portsmore, M., Paul, K. M., Moison, E. A., Kim, J., & Maltese, A. V. (2023). Characterizing engineering outreach educators' talk moves: An exploratory framework. *Journal of Engineering Education*, 112(2), 337–364.

Robertson, A. D., Scherr, R. E., & Hammer, D. (Eds.). (2016). *Responsive teaching in science and mathematics*. New York: Routledge.

van Es, E. A., & Sherin, M. G. (2008). Mathematics teachers' "learning to notice" in the context of a video club. *Teaching and Teacher Education*, 24(2), 244–276. https://doi.org/10.1016/j.tate.2006.11.005.

van Es, E. A., & Sherin, M. G. (2021). Expanding on prior conceptualizations of teacher noticing. *ZDM Mathematics Education*, 53, 17–27. https://doi.org/10.1007/s11858-020-01211-4.

5

Engineering Activities

What Counts as Engineering?

Engineering activities for K-8 students share qualities with the products and processes of professional engineers. At the most basic level, engineering activities for both youth and professionals require **a solution to a problem with criteria and constraints** drawn from the real world. Moreover, engineering problems do not have a single right answer or solution. With a variety of materials, mechanisms, constraints, and creativity, there are **multiple solutions to a problem**. While professionals may create functional designs for products such as bridges and medical devices, students often produce designs to solve smaller scale problems. However, in both cases, **the solutions need to be testable**. That is, there needs to be a way to evaluate how well the solutions solve the problems and whether they meet the criteria and constraints. Testing, whether by physical testing or feedback from users, should support iteration and refinement of the solutions. Three core ideas define engineering activities that engage students in the practices of engineering: 1) problems with criteria and constraints, 2) multiple possible solutions, and 3) solutions that are testable.

Let's look at an example of an engineering activity for students through this lens. The problem in this activity is that Sasha's food is being taken from her lunch box. The solution must meet the designated criteria to protect Sasha's food from theft. The criteria and constraints for this problem relate to the classroom. First, the students must work with the provided materials, and second, they have only two class periods to complete their designs. Under these constraints and criteria, solutions like a giant, swinging hammer to injure the thief or exploding glitter would not be considered valid. Moreover,

DOI: 10.4324/9781003378174-5

while students might propose creative ideas such as designing an intricate Rube Goldberg machine, some of these imaginative designs would not be able to be accomplished in the amount of time allotted.

Lunch Box Protector Overview

Engineering Problem

Sasha's favorite treats are being stolen from her lunch box in her fourth-grade locker.

Engineering Challenge

Create a solution to protect Sasha's lunch.

Criteria

- ★ prevent Sasha's treats from being stolen
- ★ not hurt the thief or anyone else in the class
- ★ not create a mess
- ★ fit in the lunchbox or locker space

Constraints

- ★ the materials available in the classroom
- ★ the time to complete the task (1–2 class periods)

Materials

- ★ AA batteries
- ★ bulbs
- ★ buzzers
- ★ wires
- ★ foil
- ★ pipe cleaners
- ★ felt
- ★ old lunch boxes

However, considering the available materials and time, multiple solutions could emerge. These solutions might include triggering a light bulb, sounding a buzzer, or utilizing foil to detect when the lunch box is opened. These solutions are also testable as other groups could see if the solution alerted Sasha or her teacher to the opening of the lunch box. Testing could provide feedback on whether an alarm was too quiet or if there was a way to open the lunchbox without triggering the solution.

In some ways, this hands-on lunch box activity resembles a typical science activity. However, it is fundamentally different. In a science activity, the teacher might ask the students to each build the same circuits from instructions. The students would then discuss how electricity travels through different elements as they compare complete circuits with non-functional circuits. Students in such a science discussion might engage in scientific reasoning practices, presenting evidence for their claims about how electricity moves from a battery to the buzzer or bulb. They might also demonstrate modeling practices by drawing pictures showing how the circuit elements and electrons interact. At the conclusion of the activity, the teacher leads a discussion to build a shared consensus of how the phenomenon works.

Science activities are essential for students to understand how the world works. However, engineering tasks are different and distinct. Working with open-ended problems, students engage in engineering practices like brainstorming, modeling, failure, and iteration, as they consider criteria and constraints, and test their solutions.

Summary – Engineering Activity Guidepost: Characteristics of Productive Engineering Activities

Is it an engineering activity? **Do activities meet these three criteria?**
1) The activity has a **goal or problem with criteria and constraints** for which students are creating a solution.
2) Students can create **more than one solution** to the problem.
3) Students' **solutions are testable and can inform future iterations**; they can get feedback from clients/peers or by using their solutions in the world to evaluate them.

The Practices of Engineering Activities: Design Task Framework

Activities that fulfill the engineering-specific criteria that we just discussed promote student engagement in the engineering design practices. The EDP includes design practices used to solve engineering problems, including problem scoping, researching, planning, creating, evaluating, communicating, and iterating. While professional engineers may employ all these practices while designing a solution, students rarely need to use all design practices for each engineering activity in the classroom. Only longer tasks that take several classes offer practice with all the steps in the EDP (see Figure 5.1). Depending on the nature of the problem or task, students may focus on different engineering design practices at different times. Let's look at three examples.

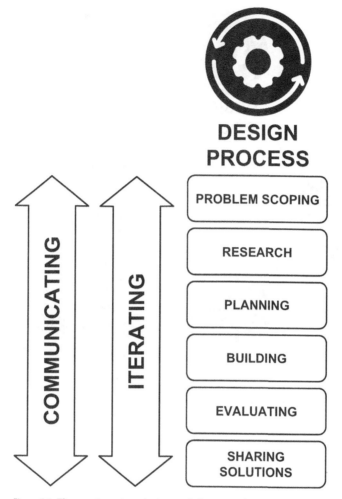

Figure 5.1 The engineering design task framework.

Example One: Wind Tube

For this challenge, students must make something that hovers in the middle of the vertical wind tube. Using multiple materials, students can quickly iterate and create at least eight different designs. The engineering graphic organizer identifies which practices students spend the most time doing in this activity—building, evaluating, or iterating. In our work in classrooms, this introductory activity supports students to see the value of iteration and failure (see Figure 5.2). They can experience firsthand how to produce a productive pathway toward a working solution. However, in this activity, students do not practice planning or problem solving because the task, constraints, and criteria are well laid-out. Examples of student solutions appear in Figure 5.3. Lesson plan and building directions are included in Appendices I and J.

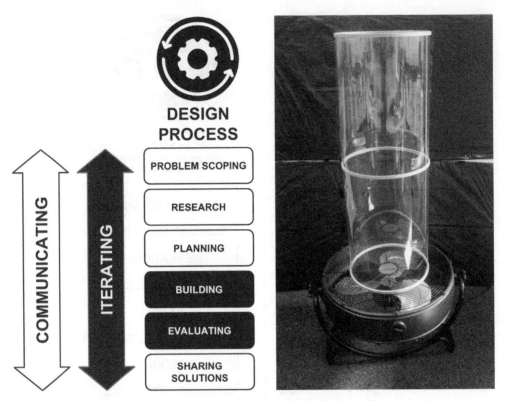

Figure 5.2 The wind tube engineering design task framework (a) and wind tube setup (b).

Figure 5.3 Student solutions for the wind tube activity.

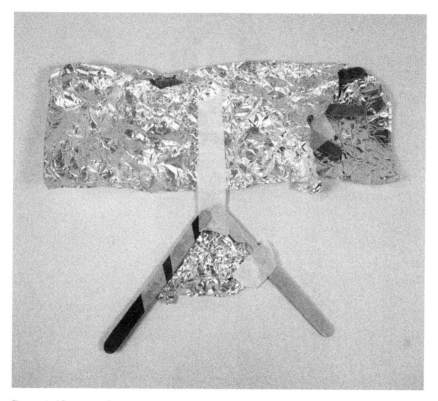

Figure 5.3 (Continued)

Example Two: Build a Backpack

In contrast, Figure 5.4 shows the engineering design task framework from a project called Novel Engineering. In Novel Engineering, students read a classroom book, identify problems faced by the characters, and then design and build a solution for a character. Students spend a significant time problem scoping as they consider constraints and criteria imposed by the book and within the classroom. Since their final goal is to build a functional prototype, the students also spend some time testing and evaluating in Novel Engineering projects.

The example in Figure 5.5 shows a backpack for two characters in *From the Mixed-Up Files of Mrs. Basil E. Frakenweiler* by E.L. Konigsburg. The characters struggled to contain their money, which was all coins. The students' solution was to create a backpack to help the characters organize the money, keep it quiet while they were hiding, and even address character disagreements about spending by dividing the backpack into two compartments (save and spend). Due to time constraints, this activity provided more opportunity for problem scoping but less for iteration and building.

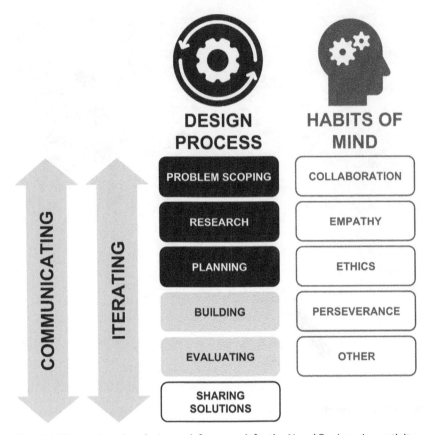

Figure 5.4 The engineering design task framework for the Novel Engineering activity.

Figure 5.5 Example solution for the Novel Engineering activity: backpack to carry clothes and money.

Example Three: The Guminator

For our third example, we will revisit the Guminator activity introduced in Chapter 1. See Figure 5.6 to see the engineering design task framework for the activity. The Guminator was part of an end of year project called "Community Inventions" that took place over multiple weeks. The fifth-grade students began the project by walking around the school talking to different people about issues in the school that they perceived to be problematic. As they identified problems to solve with engineering, they also spent time problem scoping as they considered available materials as well as the criteria and constraints specific to the problems. The teacher included a mid-design share-out where students could try each other's prototypes. The mid-design share-out was supported with a feedback sheet to help students structure feedback to be specific. After the share-out, students spent time iterating and improving their designs. Their final solutions were shared in a poster session documenting how the devices worked, emphasizing the communicating aspect of engineering.

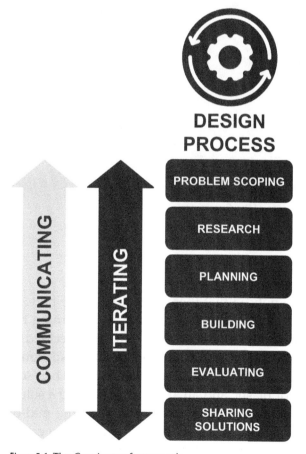

Figure 5.6 The Guminator framework.

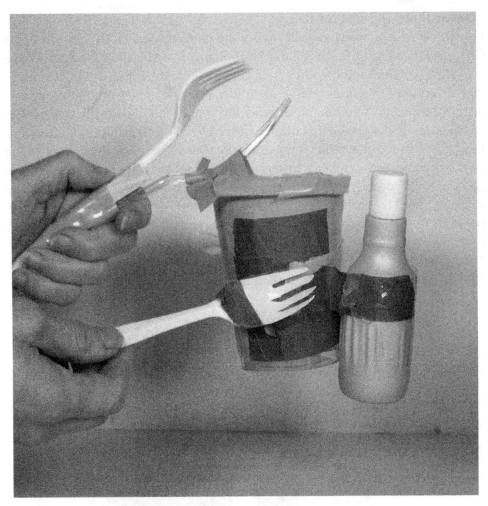

Figure 5.7 The final design of the Guminator.

Sasha and Sal noticed that there was gum on the bottom of many desks. After talking with the school janitorial staff and learning that staff only had time to clean under the desks once per year, they decided to create a device to remove the gum. Their first prototype used a plastic knife, which worked on some pieces but not on some of the older pieces. Their second version had a stronger piece of plastic and an attachment to hold a solution to soften the gum. When students tested their design during the mid-design share-out, their classmates thought the design needed a way to catch the scraped-off gum so no one had to touch it. Incorporating that feedback, Sasha and Sal built a final prototype that included an attached bin lined with a plastic bag for easy disposal.

Examining the Elements of the Design Task Framework

Each engineering activity offers students varying opportunities to practice the components of the EDP. Professional engineers often engage in all practices when working on an engineering problem. However, students are learning how to do engineering. Therefore, sometimes certain practices receive greater emphasis than others, with students spending more time on some and little or no time on others. Table 5.1 looks at the wind tube, backpack, and school

Table 5.1 Examples of Activities with Differing Levels of Structure

	Wind Tube	Backpack	Pick a Problem at Your School
PROBLEM SCOPING	Problem is defined by teacher.	Problem is defined by teacher. Students can add additional constraints/criteria.	Students pick their own problem and outline the constraints and criteria.
MATERIALS	Students are given a small selection of materials.	Students are given a selection of materials that can be used in various ways for high solution diversity.	Students have a wide selection of materials and can request other materials.
EVALUATING/ ITERATING	Everyone is required to use the same testing station.	Everyone is required to test the backpacks in the same way but might have additional tests based on student-identified individual constraints/criteria.	Students develop tests based on their specific problem/solution.
DEFINITION OF SUCCESS	Success meets constraints as defined by teacher, for instance, "Stay within the two bands for a certain amount of time."	Success meets teacher-defined constraints and criteria with student input.	Successful designs address student-defined criteria and constraints and meet the needs of users.

problem activities in terms of their emphasis on problem scoping, materials, evaluating/iterating, and definition of success.

In addition to differences in emphasis placed on the engineering design practices, activities can also vary in the amount of structure. The wind tube activity is a highly constrained and structured activity. However, on the other end of the spectrum, the Guminator activity offered less structure and fewer constraints. In fact, the prompt for this activity was simply for students to find a problem in their school and solve it. With this activity, not only were solutions different, but students were all solving different problems. No matter where activities fall on the spectrum highlighting varying levels of structure, they should allow room for students' ideas and diversity of solutions.

As you will see in the following discussions, emphasis on each component of the EDP varies according to learning goals, time constraints, or students' previous experience with materials or engineering. The first two we'll look at are communicating and iterating. These two practices happen throughout the design process as shown in Figure 5.8.

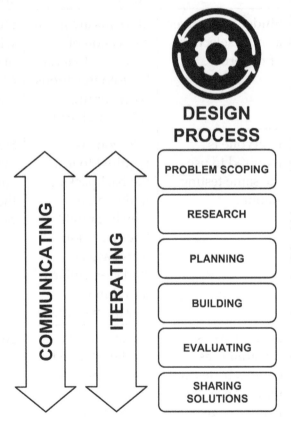

Figure 5.8 The design task framework.

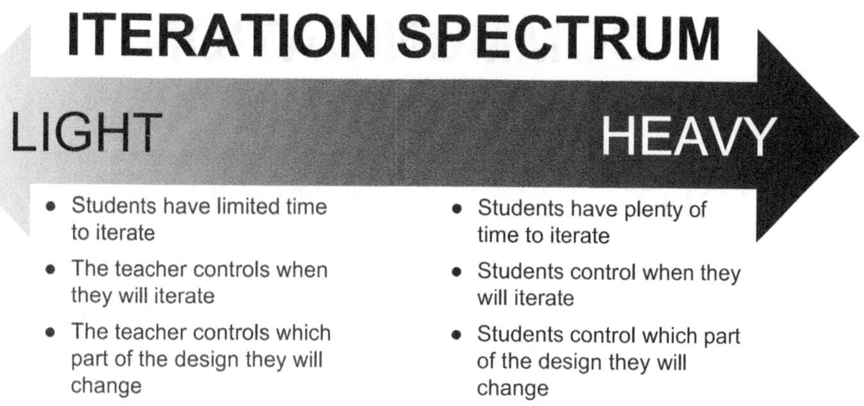

ITERATION SPECTRUM

LIGHT

- Students have limited time to iterate
- The teacher controls when they will iterate
- The teacher controls which part of the design they will change

HEAVY

- Students have plenty of time to iterate
- Students control when they will iterate
- Students control which part of the design they will change

Figure 5.9 The iteration spectrum.

Iteration

Engineers don't create a functional final design on their first try. They make changes to both their design ideas and what they create as they work. They base their iterations on additional information gathered through research, testing, and feedback. This is equally true for students who are learning engineering design practices. Students make small and large changes to their designs at different points in their processes. In the classroom, the number of iterations is based on the activities' structure and goals, time, and available materials. For example, the goal of the wind tube activity is to promote frequent and quick iterations through physical testing. In the Guminator example, the teacher encouraged students to work through several iterations. The Guminator's designers continued to iterate on their design based on feedback from their classmates, school staff, and their own design testing. Figure 5.9 shares a spectrum of possible iteration engagement in the classroom.

Communicating

Communication is key throughout the EDP. For professional engineers, the final representation and description of their design is often the most important product of their work. Professional engineers communicate with investors, manufacturing partners, and others about the specifications of their solution. The final drawings, computer models, accompanying documents, and analyses describe their design choices and process so that others can understand their ideas.

In K-12 engineering, students should also communicate about their products and processes throughout a design activity. The amount of time dedicated to communicating designs is proportional to the design activity itself: for a very short (less than one hour) design challenge, students may describe their

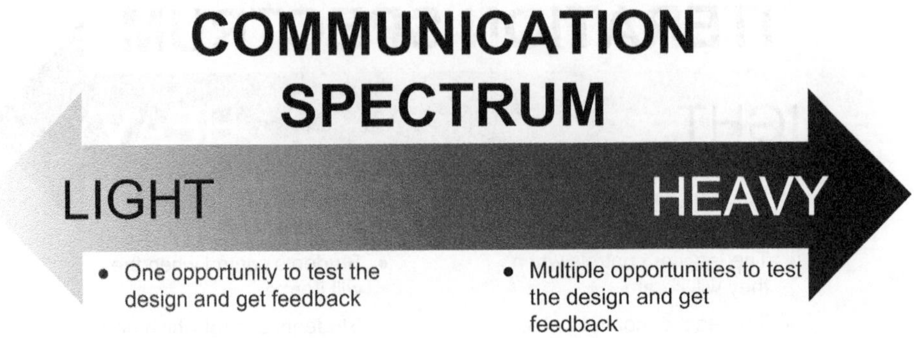

COMMUNICATION SPECTRUM

LIGHT

- One opportunity to test the design and get feedback

HEAVY

- Multiple opportunities to test the design and get feedback

Figure 5.10 The communication spectrum.

designs to a teacher as the teacher circles the room, or they may informally talk to other teams at shared testing stations, or they could do a brief share-out of their final design and process with the whole class.

A much longer project affords multiple opportunities for informal and formal communication. These opportunities may include sharing initial design ideas to get class feedback before building, or check-ins during building, or advice after testing. Other opportunities include formal feedback sessions among groups and final design presentations to visitors. When discussing their designs, students benefit from the chance to articulate their decision-making process. We have found it productive to have students focus equally on product and process: Students will naturally want to discuss their final and/or most successful design, but they should also share their design process, how they got from problem to solution. Placing value on the process shows students that that their ideas are equally as valuable as fully functioning designs. It also highlights the importance of the learning that occurs while moving through the process. Figure 5.10 details a communication spectrum.

Problem Scoping

When problem scoping, professional engineers clarify the problem that they are trying to solve. Studies of engineers show that with complex, open-ended problems, the problem and solution co-evolve; that is, working on a solution helps define the problem, and working on the problem better defines appropriate solutions (e.g., Atman et al., 2007; Atman & Turns, 2001).

When instructors provide students with well-defined problems, they are doing most of the problem-scoping work. For example, many design tasks intended for children provide criteria and constraints such as, "Build something to protect an egg when the egg is dropped from six feet. Use some tape, a box, and cotton balls as materials, and you have thirty minutes to build." In many cases, this approach is appropriate, particularly when the instructor

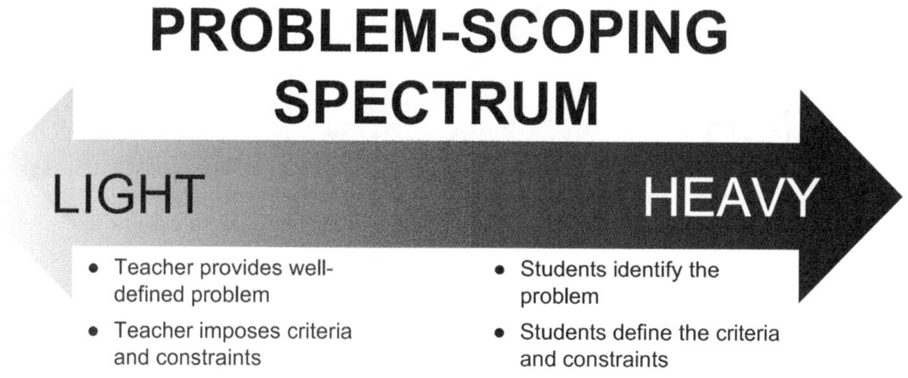

PROBLEM-SCOPING SPECTRUM

LIGHT

- Teacher provides well-defined problem
- Teacher imposes criteria and constraints

HEAVY

- Students identify the problem
- Students define the criteria and constraints

Figure 5.11 The problem-scoping spectrum.

wants to focus on other parts of the design process, such as planning or iteration within a limited amount of class time. However, in these activities, students are not getting the experience of scoping the problem themselves.

Even young students are fully capable of problem scoping. For example, kindergarteners can think about the criteria, constraints, and testing procedure for a house they will build for The Three Little Pigs. In a ten-minute, whole-class conversation they will bring up that the house needs to fit the pigs, that it needs to remain standing when the Big Bad Wolf blows on it, and that that only straw, sticks, or bricks can be used. Older students can engage in rich problem scoping, such as we saw with the Guminator, where the students found the problem and developed the criteria, constraints, and solutions. To develop problem-scoping skills, students need to both experience well-defined problems and discover their own problems. See Figure 5.11 for the problem-scoping spectrum.

Planning

Those new to engineering often assume that professional engineers plan their designs on paper or a computer, often as clearly labeled drawings, and then translate the drawn plan to a three-dimensional mock-up. In practice, though, engineers plan throughout the design process in many ways, including drawing on paper or modeling on a computer, creating lists, manipulating both prototype and final materials, and collaborating with colleagues. Several factors determine engineers' planning processes. Complex designs necessitate significant planning, while simple designs with familiar materials may require less planning. Engineers also plan different parts of a design to varying levels of detail. For example, a designer creating a solar-powered backpack may first focus solely on creating small and light solar panels and battery pieces, intentionally leaving the design of the bag, straps, and closures to a later stage.

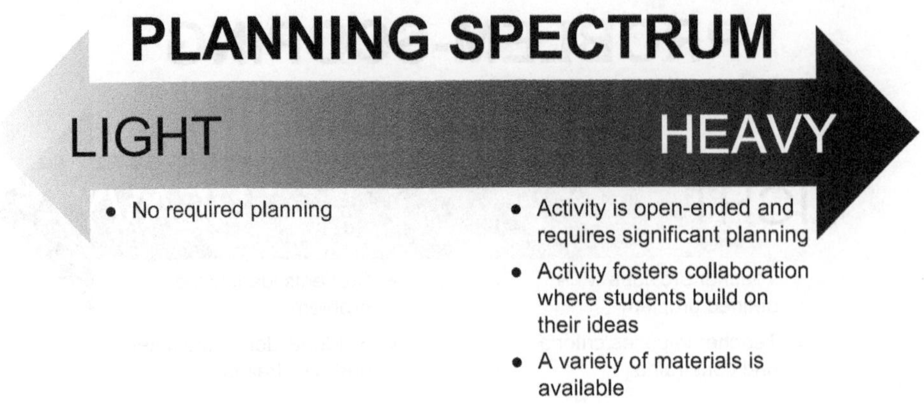

PLANNING SPECTRUM

LIGHT

- No required planning

HEAVY

- Activity is open-ended and requires significant planning
- Activity fosters collaboration where students build on their ideas
- A variety of materials is available

Figure 5.12 The planning spectrum.

While planning and drawing are not synonymous, they are strongly linked. Both planning and drawing for the purposes of communication and planning are learned practices. Throughout the design process, drawing is a common tool used to capture and communicate ideas. For students, the need for drawing and planning can vary greatly depending on the task and their experience. In the wind tube activity, planning would not have significantly helped students since they could get quick feedback from rapid building and iterations. Additionally, if students lack experience with available materials or mechanisms, formal planning and/or drawing can be difficult without prior knowledge and experiences to inform their designs. In this case, it may make more sense for them to manipulate materials when they start to plan. Likewise, if students lack drawing techniques to represent certain design elements accurately, drawing designs to communicate or plan can be futile and lead to confusion among group members.

Planning tasks should meaningfully support the design process. Formal planning may not be necessary for simple tasks, such as making a pencil holder with craft materials. In addition, planning may be less useful if students have little experience with the materials or the concept, such as in the wind tube activity. In this activity, generating ideas for building and trying these ideas in the tube took priority. By contrast, in the Novel Engineering activity, students spent more time planning since they had to think through their designs, considering the function, dimensions, materials, and characters' needs. (See Figure 5.12 for the planning spectrum.)

Research

To understand a problem, engineers gather information. The information provides insight into a client or context. Research can take several forms in

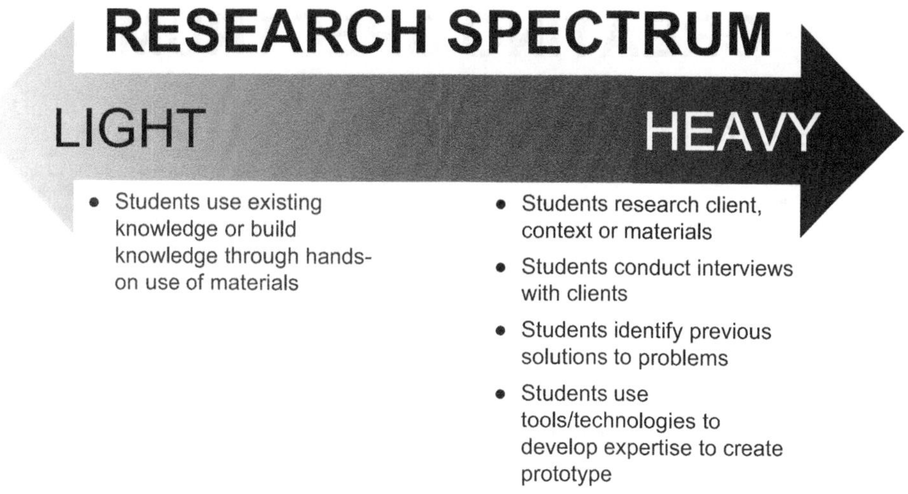

RESEARCH SPECTRUM

LIGHT

HEAVY

- Students use existing knowledge or build knowledge through hands-on use of materials

- Students research client, context or materials
- Students conduct interviews with clients
- Students identify previous solutions to problems
- Students use tools/technologies to develop expertise to create prototype

Figure 5.13 The research spectrum.

engineering design such as interviews, observations, or surveys. Additionally, before designing a new prototype, engineers look at previous solutions to a problem to see what has already been done, how it was created, and how it might be improved upon.

In the context of classroom engineering, research may be foregrounded or backgrounded depending on the goals. Some activities such as the wind tube do not require much research; students leverage existing knowledge or experiences to inform their designs. Activities such as those in Novel Engineering typically have a medium emphasis on research. In these activities, through reading, students learn about a character who will act as their client. They learn about the character's home, family, and preferences, which will inform the criteria and constraints of their design. Open-ended problems require the most research. For example, if students are solving problems in their school, such as the Guminator, they may interview stakeholders, such as school staff, or they may research potential design materials. See Figure 5.13 for the research spectrum.

Creating

When we talk about creating, we are referring to a variety of actions. We include building physical artifacts, designing processes, and making conceptual plans. Professional engineers often create full-scale, functional prototypes to see how their ideas work. They also may create smaller models for large-scale projects, bridges, or water systems that can't be prototyped at full scale. In these and many other cases, computer simulations and models have become powerful tools for exploring the functionality of designs.

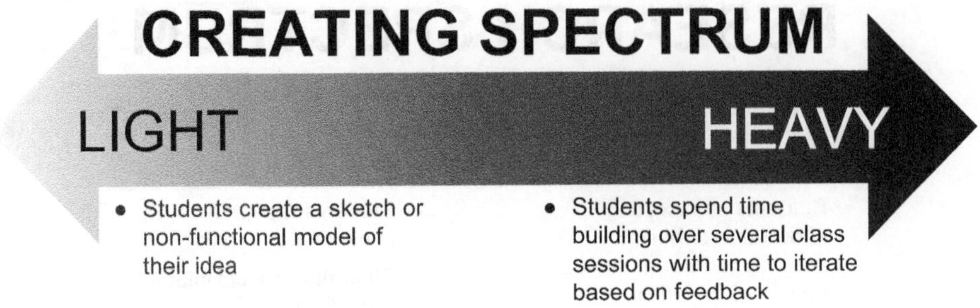

CREATING SPECTRUM

LIGHT   HEAVY

- Students create a sketch or non-functional model of their idea

- Students spend time building over several class sessions with time to iterate based on feedback

Figure 5.14 The creating spectrum.

For students, creating helps them interact with their design, test how it works, and get feedback to inform future changes. A secondary goal is to help students become proficient with the materials or tools they will use for building. Professional engineers draw on their experience to create prototypes. Students, on the other hand, are learning foundational engineering competence as they create their prototypes. Their skills in planning, creating, and building deepen with every engineering experience. Complex materials like robotics, laser cutters, and coding require students to gain experience to understand how they are used. Sometimes simple materials like tape, paper, and popsicle sticks may also be new to students in an engineering context and require time for them to explore their properties.

In K-8 classrooms, the majority of engineering activities require students to physically construct their designs. However, there are examples where young students' creating could be characterized as "light." For example, students may redesign the configuration of a city park to make space for a skate park. Students can't physically prototype the skate park, but they *can* draw the new configuration, specifying dimensions and design. Then, they can use the drawing to get feedback from peers and even city stakeholders. Activities on this end of the spectrum help students learn to identify and scope problems as well as plan with a partner or a small group. See Figure 5.14 for the creating spectrum.

Activities such as spaghetti towers or a chair for a stuffed animal fall in the middle of the creating spectrum. In these activities, students build with materials and then test and identify changes to make in future iterations, but do not develop full-scale or fully functioning "final" designs. Building functional final designs require the heaviest amount of creating. For instance, students' fabricating and programming a robot for a competition involves a lot of building and programming with multiple rounds of testing and iteration. Making a full-size cardboard chair that can hold a person is one example of a "high making" activity (High Tech High, 2024). Both activities, the robot and the chair, minimize other practices. For example, students building a full-size cardboard chair do less problem scoping because the task is well defined.

"Heavy" creating activities may often take place over several weeks or an entire semester and integrate an array of engineering practices. Planning a community garden, for example, involves in-depth problem scoping, stakeholder interviews, and site assessments as well as research to identify materials and previous solutions. Creating the final garden containers and watering system involves a significant amount of creating.

Evaluating/Testing

Engineers evaluate to gain feedback about what is working well and what may need to change. Evaluation and feedback spark ideas about how to implement changes. Feedback often comes from formal or informal physical tests, clients or users, or stakeholders or peers. Evaluation occurs throughout the design process, not only at the end, and ongoing evaluation throughout the engineering design process engages many K-12 students. Think of an egg drop, where students spend several class periods designing something to prevent their egg from breaking. However, if students have only one chance to evaluate their design, they may not be engaged, understand, or be curious about the reasons their egg survived or didn't.

Students need multiple opportunities to test their prototypes while they can still make changes. In the case of an egg drop, they might need two or three opportunities to test designs before the final test. Throughout this testing and iteration process, students' understanding of the viability of the materials and configurations deepens. In some projects, testing and iteration are informal. For example, if students are building a vehicle and need to attach an axle to allow the wheels to spin, they momentarily pause to check the wheels. In this case, they are engaged in a short evaluation phase. See Figure 5.15 for the evaluating/testing spectrum.

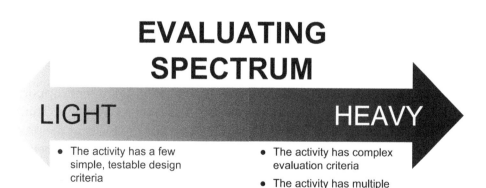

Figure 5.15 The evaluating spectrum.

In summary, light evaluation activities consist of assessing a few testable qualities of the design. A Chair for Mr. Bear asks students to evaluate, Does he fit? Does it help him sit? Does it stay together when dropped? Activities with evaluation in the middle of the spectrum require students to balance trade-offs or consider physical tests with stakeholder feedback. For example, building a toy for a child requires the prototype to physically work and for the child client to enjoy playing with it. Activities that involve heavier evaluation include multiple rounds of iteration with data collection and analysis. For example, an engineering activity that tasks students to create a device that sorts M&M's candy by color involves testing the loading mechanism storing the candy as well as the interaction between the sensors and the sorting mechanism. The amount and nature of testing and evaluation is linked to the goal of the activity itself.

Sharing Solutions

Professional engineers' final product is a set of plans that document their solution to a problem so that it can be made and produced by others. These carefully created models, drawings, and written documentation must be clear and detailed. For students learning engineering, sharing solutions can be an important component of the learning process as it can help them to reflect on how their solution worked, material properties that they discovered, and engineering design practices that supported their success. In addition, sharing solutions in a classroom helps students to learn from each other. Seeing one group's solution for an activity may support another group on a future activity.

Like the other components, sharing solutions can be something a teacher can decide to emphasize or not. For short activities like the wind tube, where the emphasis is on other engineering design practices, there may be no need for sharing as students had similar experiences and designs. On the other hand, the Guminator project had many steps and components, and groups had very different experiences. The final sharing through a poster and presentation for a large project can support students in solidifying their learning (see Figure 15.16).

This chapter offers a variety of activities that provide students opportunities to engage in the engineering design process in different ways. Thinking about the class's objectives, educators can determine the focus of the process. Starting with only a few components allows the students to build their skills by giving them enough time to practice those focus components. Gradually, the students will gain confidence with activities that include multiple components and require more independence. We'll talk about these design activity components in more detail throughout the book. The next chapter will build

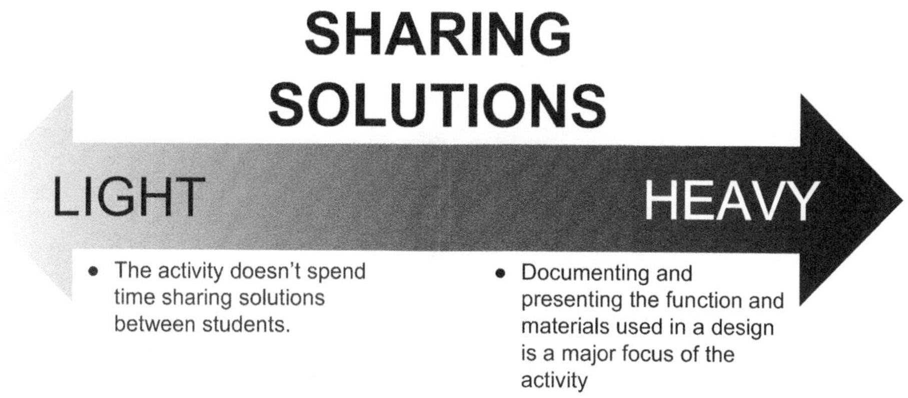

SHARING SOLUTIONS

LIGHT

HEAVY

- The activity doesn't spend time sharing solutions between students.

- Documenting and presenting the function and materials used in a design is a major focus of the activity

Figure 5.16 The sharing solutions spectrum.

on what we've discussed in this chapter and walk through an array of beginning activities

References

Atman, C. J., Adams, R. S., Cardella, M. E., Turns, J., Mosborg, S., & Saleem, J. (2007). Engineering design processes: Comparison of student and expert practitioners. *Journal of Engineering Education*, 96(4), 359–379.

Atman, C. J., & Turns, J. (2001). Studying engineering design learning: Four verbal protocol studies. In C. M. Eastman, W. M. McCracken & W. C. Newsletter (Eds.), *Design knowing and learning: Cognition in design education*. Elsevier. https://doi.org/10.1016/B978-008043868-9/50003-6.

High Tech High. (2024). *The cardboard chair exhibition*. Hthunboxed. https://hthunboxed.org/videos/the-cardboard-chair-exhibition/.

6

Getting Engineering Started in Your Classroom

In this chapter, our aim is to help teachers learn how to thoughtfully design engineering experiences for their students, whether teachers are brand new to engineering or have been incorporating engineering into their classrooms for years. We present two learning situations, following the thought processes of two teachers who teach different grade levels, have different amounts of time and learning goals, and as a result choose two very different engineering experiences for their students. By highlighting each teacher's decision-making processes, including their anticipations and justifications, we hope to show how engineering activities are not one-size-fits-all, rather, productive engineering encompasses a wide range of activities tailored to particular students and purposes.

Throughout this chapter, notice each teacher's attention to student agency in their decision making. While it is not always possible or desirable to give students complete agency over an entire engineering activity, the teachers are intentional in considering ways to give students more agency at every phase. Both teachers consciously make decisions that de-emphasize competition. While it may be the case that competition motivates some students, many students tend to feel unsuccessful, unmotivated, and less confident in competitive situations. Studies show that competition discourages and demotivates many students, in particular students from groups who have been traditionally marginalized from engineering. As a result, we recommend avoiding competition when first starting engineering activities.

We follow two teachers: a third-grade teacher, Michael, who teaches a class of students who have not begun to do engineering activities, and Vera,

DOI: 10.4324/9781003378174-6

the sixth-grade teacher we met in Chapter 3 with the turtle protection devices task. Vera's students are academically high achieving and comfortable engaging in traditional intellectually challenging tasks. They have had less experience with experiential learning and hands-on building. While Michael teaches a single class of twenty-five third-graders, Vera teaches five sections of sixth-grade science. We walk through three stages of activity design: (1) planning the activity, (2) implementing the activity, and (3) reflecting on the activity.

Planning the Activity

You'll notice that the planning stage is by far the longest! In the planning stage, we will explore the teachers' thinking around three areas: 1) goals and practical constraints; 2) choice of the design task topic (while ensuring it is truly an engineering task) including details of the task, including materials, and group composition; and 3) planning individual lessons.

Goals and Practical Constraints

Each teacher first considers their goals for the engineering experience, including not only engineering goals but classroom goals such as classroom management, standards, and social emotional learning. Goals are influenced by students' previous experiences, including with engineering. For example, the teachers reflected on the students' confidence and skills with group collaboration, physical building, and the use of different kinds of materials.

Michael's goals for his students are to 1) be excited about engineering, 2) engage in a hands-on building activity, and 3) become more comfortable with failure, which challenges those students with perfectionist tendencies. Michael has noticed that his students tend to only answer questions in front of the whole class if they are sure of the answer. He therefore is interested in finding an engineering task that will encourage public vulnerability. Michael also prefers an engineering task that can be accomplished either in small groups or individually, to offer options for students to work either alone or with others.

Vera, as a middle school science teacher, must ensure that her students meet a set of science standards over the year, so she must choose a task that aligns with that content. Vera also wants her high-achieving students to begin to think more deeply about engineering in the real world, including sociotechnical considerations. Vera is working hard on getting students to work well together in groups, so she wants a task that can only be accomplished in teams.

No learning environment has unlimited time and resources; it is important to craft engineering activities that fit within these constraints. At the very beginning of planning, teachers must consider, How much time do I have? What kinds of materials do I have access to? How much individualized support will students need for this activity?

Michael wants the first engineering activity to be short, sweet, and fun, so students are left wanting to do more engineering. He decides to do an hour-long activity and wants to ensure that a wide variety of designs are successful, so students are less likely to compare their designs with others'. He has access to simple craft and handmade materials.

Vera can be flexible with time as long as the engineering task relates directly to the prescribed science content. She decides to do a longer activity that integrates science and engineering. To ensure that students have enough time to truly engage with the topic and not feel rushed designing, she decides to create a unit that consists of about ten one-hour lessons. Vera opts for mostly recycled materials, along with necessary craft materials, to align with her commitment to sustainability.

Possible Engineering Goals

Students will:
- ★ develop proficiency with hands-on building using an array of tools and materials.
- ★ work collaboratively in teams.
- ★ experience failure in a safe environment.
- ★ build mechanistic reasoning.
- ★ balance criteria and constraints.
- ★ use feedback from users or physical testing results to make informed design changes.

Practical Classroom Constraints

- ★ time and space
- ★ material cost and student familiarization with materials
- ★ students' construction abilities
- ★ students' collaboration abilities

Academic Classroom Constraints

- ★ alignment with standards
- ★ alignment with other academic content, current events, local topics of interest

Crafting the Design Task

Once the goals and constraints are clear, teachers can start searching for or brainstorming engineering design tasks and ideas by searching online, checking in books, and talking with peers. Like engineering design itself, designing the design task is also an iterative process! The goals and practical constraints of the design activity may not change, but smaller decisions (materials, how to test, etc.) for an activity can and should be revisited as the activity is fleshed out. As you learned in the last chapter, engineering design challenges are typically defined by a problem or goal, criteria and constraints, and testing procedure (and/or definition of success/failure), and these need to be internally consistent.

Authentic engineering questions: As described in Chapter 5, to ensure an activity is truly engineering and not, for example, a craft exercise or a puzzle, we can ask three questions: Is there more than one possible solution? Are solutions testable? Is there a clear goal or do solutions solve a problem?

Reminder: What Makes an Activity Engineering?

Engineering design tasks are defined by

- ★ **a problem or goal**: What is the problem and for whom?
- ★ **criteria**: What does the design need to do?
- ★ **constraints**: What are the limitations? (Often this includes time and materials.)
- ★ **testing process**: How will we test our designs to see if they meet the criteria?

Goal, criteria, constraints, and testing process need to be consistent with each other!

Authentic engineering questions:

- ★ Is there more than one possible solution?
- ★ Are solutions testable?
- ★ Is there a clear goal or do solutions solve a problem?

Michael decides to do a wind tube design challenge, which he experienced at a science museum. He knows he will have to create the testing apparatus and find appropriate fans, which seems doable. He plans to give students a wide range of craft materials to make something that hovers in the tube above the fan. The criteria, constraints, and testing process for this task are straightforward. The students will design something that fits inside the tube and hovers for a set length of time, anywhere from five to ten seconds. With thirty minutes of building and testing time, Michael is confident his students can succeed with a five-second hover challenge, but he is prepared to be flexible with this goal. This task definitely meets the guidelines for an authentic engineering question: There is a clear goal, it allows more than one solution (and is likely to generate many diverse solutions), and it is absolutely testable. While some engineering tasks include a real-world problem with a client to be solved, that is not necessary for this task, which is more focused on building engineering practices. Michael's main goals are for students to enjoy doing the activity and feel excited and confident about engineering. Therefore, he is not concerned that this task lacks an authentic client or context.

Vera decides to align with the sixth-grade chemistry standards, specifically the standards related to exothermic chemical reactions. She finds an appropriate design challenge from Hereau et al. (2021) that she thinks she can build on to be more open-ended and last longer. In the OpenSciEd version, students are tasked with evaluating different sea turtle egg incubator designs, with the goal of keeping the eggs at 29 °C. If sea turtle eggs incubate above this temperature, they hatch female, and below this temperature, they hatch male. Climate change has resulted in increased beach temperatures, which has led to a majority of sea turtles hatching as females. Vera decides to extend this task beyond temperature and ask students to design a portable transport device. By adding transport criteria, the task becomes more than simply creating an incubator: Students must also create a portable container to protect the eggs from breaking.

Vera begins to sketch the activity flow to ensure that this real-world problem will lead to an open-ended design challenge. First, students will experiment with different quantities of calcium chloride, hydrogen peroxide, and water to create an exothermic reaction in a plastic bag, which can be placed next to the model turtle eggs. While this part of the design challenge feels highly constrained, Vera can imagine that the other aspects of the designs—how to insulate and protect the eggs and how to carry them—could be more student directed. At this point, Vera has a general idea of the task and can begin defining the activity.

Problem/Goal

In this egg task, the problem and goal are clear: transporting the eggs and keeping them at a consistent temperature.

Criteria, Constraints, and Testing Procedure

Vera has conducted many engineering design challenges in the past, in all of which she, as the teacher, determined the criteria, constraints, and testing procedure ahead of time. She has been wanting to give some of this agency to her students and decides this engaging activity is a perfect opportunity. She plans to have the whole class engage in authentic problem scoping, which involves deciding on the criteria, the constraints, and the testing procedure. Because the students will define the final criteria, constraints, and testing procedure, at this stage Vera spends some time anticipating what students may decide. The criteria will include keeping the right temperature and not breaking the eggs. Vera anticipates that students may want to add other criteria like the number of eggs a device holds and how easy it is to use.

While Vera wants to give her students as much agency as possible, she will still need to impose some practical classroom constraints, such as the number of days to build as well as the overall size of the designs as storage space is limited. While Vera is committed to sustainability and would prefer using only recycled materials, she decides to leave that up to the students. Thinking about the testing procedure, Vera anticipates that students will propose chicken eggs for testing, but she is worried about students' designs getting covered in egg after failed tests. However, she wants to ensure that there is a way to tell if the designs are protecting the eggs well. She decides to bring the problem of how to test to the students and see if they can create a reasonable test. While leaving this to the students makes her nervous, she reminds herself that even if they spend time on it and cannot come up with a better testing process than simply using hard-boiled eggs, it will not be wasted time.

Is there more than one possible solution?

Yes, Vera can envision a number of different designs students could create even with the necessary constraints.

Are solutions testable? Is there a clear goal?

One design goal is keeping a certain temperature, which is definitely testable. While Vera is not yet sure how students will test their designs for protection, she is confident there is a way to test.

Table 6.1 Materials for Michael's Classroom

Structural	Connecting	Floating	Other	Recyclable
• Straws • Popsicle sticks • Skewers • Cups • Paper plates • Cardboard	• Tape • Paper clips • Binder clips • String Rubber bands	• Plastic bags • Foil • Wax paper • Tissue paper • Paper	• Tools: scissors & hole punches • Weight: pennies or weights	• Egg cartons • Empty yogurt cups • Toilet paper

Material Selection and Group Configurations

Michael chooses the wind tunnel task because it works well with craft and everyday materials, as outlined in Table 6.1, and does not require many tools. He does not want students to have to use anything more than scissors and tape. Regarding materials, he has the following objectives: 1) enough for students to work individually or in groups and to make multiple design attempts, 2) enough variety to inspire creativity and innovation, and 3) easily manipulated and familiar. Michael offers a materials table for the whole class to share instead of creating individual student kits.

Michael decides to have his students work in pairs rather than small groups since the design is small and the children have not had a lot of experience with small group work. He also decides it is fine if students work individually, as in parallel play, as long as they share ideas with their partner. Michael decides to create pairs based on the current seating arrangement, since those students know each other already.

Vera anticipates that the designs will be small enough to fit on one desk but big enough to hold about four eggs, with a variety of insulating and cushioning materials. She decides to collect and provide small shoe boxes for the designs as that will make stacking designs possible for storage. Since these students are in sixth grade and can use more tools safely, Vera allows hot glue and adult scissors to make construction easier. Vera categorizes the materials as seen in Table 6.2, knowing that all of these ideas, especially the testing materials, are subject to change when students engage in problem scoping themselves. In addition to the materials preparation for the egg protectors, Vera prepares the ingredients each group needs to create the chemical reaction to test the temperature: calcium chloride, hydrogen peroxide, water, measuring spoons, small plastic bags, and a thermometer.

Table 6.2 Materials for Vera's Classroom

Structural	Connecting	Cushioning/ Insulating	Tools	Recyclable
• Straws • Popsicle sticks • Pipe cleaners • Skewers • Cardboard	• Tape • Paper clips • Binder clips • String • Rubber bands • Hot glue	• Packing materials • Fluff: felt, foam, packing peanuts • Tissue paper	• Scissors • Hole punch • Glue gun	• Egg cartons • Small shoe boxes • Plastic eggs or chicken eggs for testing?

Because she has five sections of students and limited storage space, Vera needs to create larger groups of four students each to ensure that she has enough space to store the designs as students progress. Vera will choose groups in advance and make a seating chart that corresponds to those groups for the entire unit. Students are used to this approach, and it avoids the social difficulties of middle schoolers choosing their own groups.

Material Selection

When selecting materials, ensure that:
★ there are enough for each group to use several different materials.
★ there is enough variety to support a successful open-ended task.
★ students are familiar with the materials or are given time to get familiar.
★ the materials are safe.

Group Considerations

When creating groups, ensure that:
★ there is enough work for each student in the group.
★ the designs are physically large enough to involve each group member.
★ for groups of more than two or three, there are designs with multiple components to be worked on simultaneously.
★ for multi-day activities, groups are larger than pairs to ensure that students don't end up alone or moving to an established group.

Rule of thumb: groups of 1–2 for up to 2nd grade, then groups of about 3 until middle school.

Table 6.3 Lesson Phases and Planning Considerations

Lesson Plan Phase	Consideration
Problem introduction	Way to introduce the problem
Mid-design check-in	Prompts for in-progress discussions or feedback
Wrap-up	Facilitation of end-of-project sharing and reflection
Scaffolds	Individual and group support needed for each phase
Assessment	Formal and/or informal approaches

Lesson Planning

While Michael's engineering activity will only be one, one-hour lesson and Vera's is about ten days, they have similar considerations while lesson planning, as illustrated in Table 6.3.

Michael decides not to make the problem scoping stage open ended; he will simply tell the students what the task is to maximize building and testing time for this task. In his verbal introduction, he will include a brief safety talk about the materials.

Michael plans to have a mid-design discussion focusing on a common design challenge about which students can brainstorm solutions. He finds a time in his schedule with enough flexibility to be able to continue the activity until each group has created at least one successful design. He plans to assist groups who need it at the very end, so that every student feels successful. He also plans on ten minutes for a final discussion and reflection.

First, each group will publicly test each of their designs, including ones that did not pass the hover test. To encourage sense-making across designs, he will collect all of the successful designs on one table for students to look at all together. His goal for the final discussion is to encourage students to start thinking mechanistically, focusing on why designs work (or not). He plans to ask students, "I wonder why these designs worked when some others and earlier iterations didn't work. Does anyone have any ideas?" He anticipates that students will talk mostly about weight and about how they created designs that were not too heavy or too light, but he will also be listening for ideas related to wind or air pushing up on the designs. While he is not overly concerned with meeting standards in this task, he is still aware

of the third-grade force and motion standards and is considering ways to come
back to this task when he begins those
lessons.

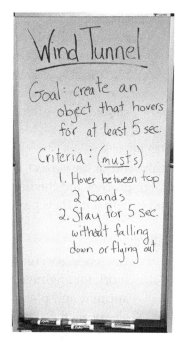

To scaffold the activity, Michael creates
an anchor poster with the design challenge statement to help students understand the challenge (Figure 6.1). He is
careful not to refer to any specific type
of flying machine, such as hovercrafts,
which could limit creativity.

As **Vera**'s task is much longer and
includes other content goals, the lesson
planning is more involved. She had
to decide which to introduce first, the
design problem or the chemistry lessons
on exothermic reactions needed for the
activity. If students learn the chemistry
first, the problem scoping will be more
straightforward, but if she introduces the
design problem, they will be motivated

Figure 6.1 Wind tube problem
definition scaffold.

to learn about exothermic reactions since they will need this chemistry to solve the problem. The first year Vera taught this unit, she
opted to do the chemistry lessons first as she was still working out
the design task ideas. In following years, she started with the design
problem and prefers that approach.

Problem Introduction

Vera decides to give students agency in the problem scoping for this
task. She describes the problem with pictures on slides as a visual
aid. She crafts a problem statement: "After a hurricane, you and
other disaster rescue volunteers found turtle egg nests near a Flori-
da beach. You decide to transport the eggs to a conservation center
and realize you need a safe container to do so. You will design, test,
modify, and optimize a portable incubator that can keep the turtle
eggs at the optimal temperature of 29 °C. This temperature will
ensure that the eggs hatch into a balanced ratio of turtle females
and turtle males. Your device will use a chemical reaction to reach
and maintain the ideal temperature." Vera then plans to facilitate a
whole-class discussion to specify criteria and constraints.

Mid-design Check-in

Vera wants students to interact across groups to learn from each other's design work. She decides to do this as a peer feedback session; she will pair two groups, who will take turns sharing a problem they are having and asking for advice from the other team. Vera decides this feedback session should come after each group has tested their design at least once.

Wrap-up

At the end of the project, the groups will give a formal presentation about their design process and the final design. The students will use a rubric that **Vera** created to help with their presentations (see Table 6.4 for the turtle protector rubric).

Scaffolds

For the ten-lesson unit, scaffolds that **Vera** uses for science lessons will work for engineering as well. She typically leads classes with slides for support and plans to use that approach for this unit. After each class, she posts the slides on Google Classroom for students to review and to allow any students who missed class to see exactly what occurred. She will create data tracking worksheets for testing the exothermic reaction materials and tracking results. Students will use their usual science notebooks for this unit; Vera plans on creating specific prompts for them to respond to in their notebooks before each class.

Assessment

Vera is using the design task as a project-based assessment for the chemistry unit. Because of this, it is important that she create opportunities for students to describe how they chose the heating materials, their designs, and their processes.

Lesson Planning

Problem Introduction: How to introduce the problem

★ For short tasks, a single 1-page or 1-slide design brief may be enough.

Mid-design: What sort of in-progress discussions or feedback will you include?

★ whole-class discussion vs. small groups
★ discuss each design vs. common issues the teacher sees

Wrap-up: What sort of discussions/feedback—share work and reflection

★ What scaffolds will students need to be successful?
★ assessment

Table 6.4 Turtle Egg Protector Project Rubric

Expectation	Beginning	Developing	Meets Expectation
PART 1-A Diagram of the final design	Diagram of the device with no labels, arrows, and/or a key	Diagram of the device is missing one or more of the following: labels, arrows, and/or a key	Diagram of the device includes labels, arrows, headings, and/or a key and materials list
	2 points	5 points	7-8 points
PART 1-B Function of the materials used	The choice of materials seems random	The choice of materials is not explained clearly	The choice of at least three materials is deliberate and clearly explained
	1 point	2 points	3 points
PART 2 Flameless heater explained with data	Data is insufficient to support the explanation	Data is recorded but not used to explain the reaction	Quantitative and qualitative data are presented in a graph or a table to support the explanation
	2 points	4 points	7 points
PART 3 Testing and improving	No improvement	Improvements without considering the self-assessment	Improvement is clearly based on evaluation matrix and the survey
	1 point	2 points	4 points
PART 4 Reflection	Some strengths of the design are described	Some strengths of the design are described. Some improvements are suggested	Strengths and weaknesses of the design are explained in detail
	1 point	3 points	5 points

Implementing the Activity

Introducing the Activity

Since engineering is often a new experience for students in K-8, expectations around what engineering is and is not need to be clear. Using language tailored to their students, both teachers made the following expectations clear:

- There is no one right answer in engineering! There are many possible ways to create a successful design.
- Iteration is a key part of engineering! The first design is almost never successful. In engineering, we create something, test it out and see how it performs, make changes to improve that performance, and repeat until we are satisfied. This process often takes multiple cycles!

A Note on Failure

★ Designs often fail in the first attempt! Failure is part of professional engineering all the way down to preschool engineering. It is a feature of engineering and does not mean the designer did anything wrong in their engineering process.

★ Students need to be prepared for designs to not work right away. It is helpful to show students a real-life example of a product that has gone through many iterations before it worked.

★ It is not critical to use the word "failure" with students; it's fine to respond to an unsuccessful test with, "Darn, I guess that didn't work." It is also important not to call failures "mistakes". A mistake implies that an event was preventable, but an engineering failure is not preventable; in fact, it's the only way to know whether something works or not!

Michael introduced the wind tunnel task as he planned, with the chart and referencing the testing station. Since the oral description took less than five minutes, he decided to quickly demonstrate the two ways a design could fail the test. He turned on the fan, grabbed a piece of foil, and asked students to predict what would happen when he dropped it in; students correctly predicted it would fly out the top, which he then confirmed. He repeated the demonstration with an empty cup, which fell straight to the bottom. Satisfied that his students understood the task, he reviewed the safety rules and sent them off to work.

Vera had previously held engineering activities with her students where the criteria and constraints were already defined. As a result, Vera wasn't surprised to notice that her students were trying to guess what Vera wanted them to say for what criteria and constraints to use. Since Vera aimed to build student agency, she tried to disrupt their guessing approach by using students' own language on the slides and accepting all ideas. Through this, Vera showed that her students' ideas were critical for problem scoping. In the sections where students did not readily offer ideas, Vera modeled the process by citing her other sections, for example by saying, "In the other class, they felt strongly that we should *only* use recycled materials in our designs. How do you all feel about that criterion?" This move also had the added benefit of creating consistency across her five sections, making Vera's job a bit easier. Vera wrote down the students' ideas of criteria and constraints on an anchor chart that was posted on the wall as shown in Table 6.5.

With the goal, criteria, and constraints chosen, the students now needed to determine the test for adequate protection of the eggs. While Vera thought dropping the designs from waist height was adequate and realistic, the students were unanimously in favor of dropping the designs in the stairwell. Vera acquiesced and wrote down the test of surviving a fall of one flight of stairs. The final piece to figure out was how to know if the turtle eggs were damaged in the drop test. Vera was surprised to discover that many students opposed using chicken eggs for testing for ethical reasons. As a result, she decided that all classes would use plastic eggs.

Table 6.5 Criteria and Constraints for the Turtle Protector

Criteria	Constraints
• Optimal temperature (29 °C) • Uses a chemical reaction as a heating element • Safe packaging of the egg (damage protection) • Safe to use • Simple design • Portable • Ventilated • Built with recycled materials • EXTRA: Easy egg pickup	• Size (must fit into a one-gallon Ziploc bag) • Time (two days in-class time to build) • Common, household reaction materials: calcium chloride, water, baking soda

As part of the final problem-scoping class period, the students brainstormed to figure out how they could use these plastic eggs for their tests, since the plastic eggs are much sturdier than real eggs. One class had the idea to put something fragile inside the plastic egg that would break if handled too roughly. They agreed they needed something fragile, cheap, and not harmful when broken like glass. Another section came up with the idea of using graphite sticks that go in refillable pencils. Vera was thrilled with this idea, as it met all her own criteria and was not something she felt she could have come up with on her own. The other sections agreed with this idea.

Designing, Building, and Testing

Once students understand the problem, criteria, and constraints (at least the initial version of criteria and constraints, these may evolve in some tasks), they can begin their individual or group design work. This work involves a number of activities such as physically constructing and testing designs, drawing plans, and investigating barely functioning prototypes. In both Vera's and Michael's tasks, the students physically construct full-scale designs. While students design, build, and test in their groups, the teachers circulate, observing, asking questions, and providing support customized to each group. While some groups might need only a simple check-in, other groups may need more hands-on support. This is particularly true in younger grades, where students are still working on fine motor skills.

> Michael realizes that some groups begin testing materials immediately to see how they function in the wind tube. Michael reinforces this productive approach and points out this approach to the whole class encouraging all students to watch and learn from these test results. Michael planned thirty minutes for building and testing. After about ten minutes, he notices a few groups have not started testing anything. These groups are intent on creating a "finished" design, and at least one team member is resistant to testing anything that still needs work.
>
> Noting the time, Michael reminds those groups who have not yet tested to do so very soon. The time reminder motivated most of the groups to test their "incomplete" designs. Finally, there is only one team that has not tested. Michael listens to these students and realizes that their reluctance is due to social friction. The two students are each committed to their own idea and have used the time to argue for their own ideas rather than build. Michael explains that both ideas sound interesting and that in engineering there is no way to know what works until it is tested. He allows them to create their

own designs as long as they promise to help each other with the construction when either needs another set of hands.

Vera's students get right to work, sketching and describing ideas and perusing materials. Vera quickly learns that while her students have not had many opportunities to make physical designs in class, they are familiar with building techniques. They quickly request sharper scissors and hot glue, which Vera provides after a brief safety lesson.

Vera quickly encounters the opposite problem from the one Michael faced. Her students want to constantly test their partially completed designs, but the testing procedure requires them to leave the classroom and go to the stairwell. Unfortunately, some teachers complained about the students' behavior during this unsupervised testing, so Vera has to accompany the students for each test. As a result, groups have to wait to test at the stairs until every group is ready, so they can all go together with Vera. Since the groups work at different speeds, they only get to "drop-test" their designs twice, but nearly all groups succeed by the second test.

Vera then notices the designs are converging and becoming more like each other with each class period. Since everyone tested at the same time, the less successful groups might have decided to copy features of the successful designs instead of figuring out ways to improve their own designs. Vera decides to use the mid-design feedback session to address this situation.

Mid-Design Check-in

Michael's lesson is only one hour, so he plans for a five-minute mid-design check-in. About 2/3 of the way through the building time, he tells students to pause work on their designs. He wants the students to use the check-in to see how well their various designs work. He has them take a sticky note and write the number of seconds their design hovered in the last test. Students put that sticky note next to their designs and then engage in a two-minute silent gallery walk, where they walk around the classroom and look at everyone's designs, noting how successful each was. Then he transitions to a short whole-class discussion. Michael asks the students to share a problem that they'd like help with. After a few students share, a common theme of balance surfaced. One group's design is constantly flipping over, and Michael has this group ask for advice from other students. One student shares a tip to cut their strings all to the same length before attaching them rather than doing one at a time. Michael had originally intended to elicit many ideas, but the first idea stated was easy to understand and likely to help many students, so he ends the discussion and they get back to work.

Vera had ten lessons planned for the entire design challenge, so she was able to use a full class period for a mid-design check-in. She structured this as a peer feedback session. First, on the day before the mid-design check-in, she gave each group a self-evaluation rubric to score their own designs and identify areas they needed to work on (see Table 6.6 for a self-evaluation rubric). Then, on the mid-design check-in day, she paired up teams to share their designs with each other and get feedback. During the first class's section, Vera realized that the students needed more structure. Some teams listed so many problems from their self-evaluation that it made it difficult for the partner team to decide where to help. Other teams only shared the working parts of their designs and then were upset when the partner team pointed out areas that needed work.

Vera decided to change the structure for the next section. She asked each team to decide together on only one aspect of their design for which they wanted peer feedback. She then modeled the peer feedback process, choosing one team to share their problem with the whole class. For the team that wanted help with their handle, Vera summarized the issue and opened it up to the rest of the class for advice. Multiple students had ideas for different handle configurations and the presenting team seemed inspired by these ideas. Then Vera paired up teams and had them take turns sharing their one troublesome aspect and getting advice from the other team. One group's design can be seen in Figure 6.2.

Wrapping up the Activity

Michael wrapped up the activity with a whole-class sense-making discussion looking across different designs. He had students collect all their tested designs, not just the design that performed the best. He had them place each design on a long table in rough order of least to most time the design hovered. Including many designs and physically separating them from the creators helped orient the discussion to focus on the designs rather than the creators. Michael then asked a general question about performance: "Why do you think these designs [pointing to one end of the table] hovered for longer than these designs [pointing to the other end of the table]." Students initially wanted to claim ownership and share their entire process, but Michael was interested in hearing students reason and analyze, so he responded by re-orienting the class to the focus question *why*. After a few turns, students started to give mechanistic reasons for the differences in the designs: Some were heavier, others were lighter; another was able to

Figure 6.2 Turtle egg protector example.

catch the wind. Some students referred to how designs looked like re-al-world objects that were good at hovering, such as a hot air balloon. Michael was thrilled to hear all the ideas students shared regarding design structure and function. He concluded the discussion comment-ing on the kind of thinking they were doing, connecting their thinking processes to the kinds of thinking engineers do.

Vera had her students create a short report and presentation about their projects. The reports focused on the scientific concepts of exothermic reactions and their engineering design processes, such as how they had made decisions as a team and how they had decided what to change between iterations. For this group of students who felt undue pressure to be constantly high achieving, Vera wanted to keep the focus on the process, rather than the success of the final product.

Table 6.6 Turtle Protector Project Self-Evaluation

Directions:				
1) Evaluate your design against the following criteria: 1 = not yet 2 = almost 3 = a definite yes				
2) Add the points to get your final score.				
3) Redesign and reevaluate your design. Your team should have 2 evaluations completed.				
Criteria	**Eval 1**	**Eval 2**	**Eval 3**	**Eval 4**
Size (not larger than 8 × 6 × 4)	yes no	yes no	yes no	yes no
Safe packaging of the egg (SHAKE test)	1 2 3	1 2 3	1 2 3	1 2 3
Portable (comfortable to carry)	1 2 3	1 2 3	1 2 3	1 2 3
Simple design (steps to build it will be easy)	1 2 3	1 2 3	1 2 3	1 2 3
Safe to use	1 2 3	1 2 3	1 2 3	1 2 3
Ventilated	1 2 3	1 2 3	1 2 3	1 2 3
Made with environmentally sustainable materials (recycled or recyclable materials)	1 2 3	1 2 3	1 2 3	1 2 3
Materials are cheap and easy to get	1 2 3	1 2 3	1 2 3	1 2 3
Design is reusable	1 2 3	1 2 3	1 2 3	1 2 3
Reaches the optimal temperature range (near the egg) of 27–30 °C	yes no 3 1			
OPTIONAL: Safe packaging of the egg (DROP test)	1 2 3	1 2 3	1 2 3	1 2 3
BONUS FEATURES (1 point for each of the features): a tool for easy egg pick-up, multipurpose, temperature can be adjusted as needed, sounds of ocean, aesthetically pleasing design				
Final score (add up the points):				

Ideas to Structure Engineering Design Sense-Making Discussions
- ★ Find two or more similar-performing designs that function differently and ask students to reason about why.
- ★ Find two or more similar-looking designs that perform very differently and ask students to reason about why.
- ★ Identify a change a group made that did not have the desired effect on the design performance and try to figure out together why that might have happened.

Reflecting on the Activity

After the design challenge was complete, the teachers reflected on the experience and took notes for the next time. Their reflection questions included the following:

- ◆ Where and how can I give students more agency?
- ◆ What additional or changes to scaffolds would be helpful?
- ◆ What changes might I make to materials, group size, or structure and timing?

Michael recalled how much faster the introduction to the activity was than he had expected and noted that for next time. Reflecting on the groups who were reluctant to test, Michael decided he needs to add something explicit to have students test earlier. Next time he will give each group or student one unaltered material, like a cup or piece of cardboard, to test in the wind tube before building in groups. He's hopeful that this public, whole-group testing experience will get all students interacting with the test from the beginning and show that testing is not only intended for "finished" designs. Finally, he wrote in his notes to schedule additional time for the mid-design sharing activity, which felt like a productive activity that encouraged students to interact with each other about their designs.

Vera was impressed with her students' ability to problem scope. Giving students authentic agency made her realize how competent her students were. The ways students were able to design the activity according their values, for example by not using chicken eggs, highlighted for Vera just how often she imposed her choices and values on students without their input. Vera also reflected on the difficult part of whole-class problem scoping: managing disagreements across students. For example, some students wanted to use only environmentally friendly materials, while others wanted to use bubble wrap because it was so effective. She decided that next year she will try out a modified approach: All groups will have to follow the general criteria and constraints chosen by the whole class, but smaller decisions like using environmentally friendly materials will be up to each group. Reflecting on the science content, she noticed gaps in understanding key science concepts relating to insulators and conductors. For example, many students wanted to use aluminum foil in their designs "because it gets hot" without understanding that it would conduct the heat away from the eggs. However, as this was part of the grade-level standards, it was critical that the students understand the difference.

While both teachers think about what they would like to change based on this first implementation, they also know that the activity must adapt in many small ways from year to year. Students' comfort and confidence with materials, group work skills, and engineering practices and routines will vary each year, requiring creativity and flexibility in planning and implementing engineering activities.

Reference

Hereau, H., McGill, T., Affolter, R., Friend, A., Gasper, S., McCleary, M., Stennett, B., Wright, W., Donna, J., Novak, M., Van Horne, K., Merritt, J., Smolek, T.J., Webb, A., Krenek, C., Brown, H., & Fortus, D. (2021). Open SciEd Unit 7.2: How can we use chemical reactions to solve a design problem? https://www.opensced.org/instructional-materials/7-2-chemical-reactions-energy/

7

A First Step: A Beginning Classroom Activity

In this chapter, we will present a case study of a launching activity used to introduce engineering and highlight the ways students engage in different phases of the engineering design process. In this activity, students build a chair for a stuffed animal that is unable to sit up by itself. We often use this activity to introduce the concepts of requirements, constraints, testing, and iteration. Through the case study, we'll address how to present the activity and materials, how to get students started, and how to structure design share-outs. We'll also discuss different ways that students can share their ideas and their work at multiple points throughout the engineering design process.

Purpose of an Introductory Activity

Introductory activities are not only used as initial engineering building experiences but are also used to introduce students to the EDP. Conversations about norms and routines are often part of these introductory experiences. Introductory activities can focus on all phases or only a part of the EDP. An activity may also address a specific set of skills for more targeted, in-depth practice. Introductory activities should be relatively low stakes, so students feel comfortable taking chances, exploring, and failing safely. Depending on the instructional goals, activities can be very open-ended or constrained. Figure 7.1 gives examples of activities with different levels of structure.

DOI: 10.4324/9781003378174-7

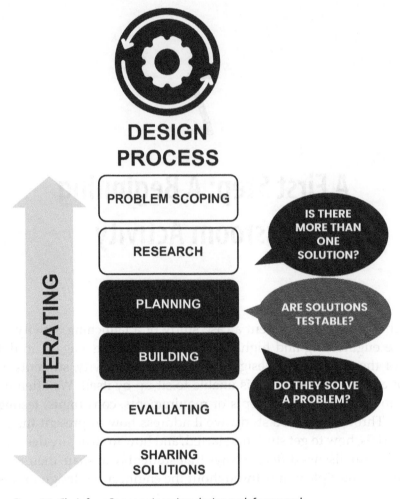

Figure 7.1 Chair for a Bear engineering design task framework.

Chair for a Bear Case Study

To illustrate an introductory activity, we are going to look at an implementation of the Chair for a Bear activity in a fourth-grade classroom. In this activity, students build a sturdy chair for a stuffed animal. We have a battery of stuffed bears that we use. (See Appendix N for lesson plan.) We've done this activity with students from kindergarten to college. It works with a variety of materials. In some classes, we've used interlocking building blocks, and in other classes, students have built with recyclable and craft materials. The chair is the design focus in this activity. Since all students understand chairs and how they work, they can readily contribute to conversations when the activity begins.

Activity Overview

In this activity, we want students to be able to identify both client-based design and basic aspects of design, or "form follows function." In client-based design, the students build with a specific client in mind. In more basic designing, students do not have a client; the main goal is functionality. Students will identify how the chair should serve the client and base their design decisions around the client's needs. Students will also gain an understanding of testing, criteria, and iteration as they build and test their chairs for functionality. Additional features such as a reclining back or cupholder can be included if students choose. We use stuffed animals that are approximately eight inches tall and are not able to stay in a seated position without support. Students are told that the chair should be sturdy and support the stuffed animal as it sits so it does not slump.

Case Study

We've done this activity with a wide range of ages. For this case study, we are going to look at Amy's fourth-grade classroom. The class had talked about engineering and had already done the wind tube activity. Amy decided to do the Chair for a Bear next because she wanted the students to get more practice with core engineering skills such as building with available materials, testing to fuel iteration, and designing for someone else. She also wanted students to practice working with a partner or small group and managing the frustration that often comes with collaborative work.

Planning for Implementation

In planning, she thought about four categories: time, materials, anticipated conversations and questions, and scaffolds for students who need additional support.

Time

Amy thought about how long the activity would take and mapped out the activity into four sessions as outlined in Table 7.2. She wanted to remain flexible and add or subtract a session depending on how quickly the students worked.

Materials

Amy considered two types of materials: 1) interlocking building bricks and 2) recyclable/craft materials. Interlocking building bricks presented two advantages: They were easily reconfigured, and many students had experience using them. However, she ultimately decided to use recyclable materials for two compelling reasons. First, not all students had experience with

Table 7.2 Chair for a Bear Tasks by Session

Session	Activity	Approximate Time
SESSION 1	Introduce activity & materials to students	15 minutes
	Planning & materials tour	15 minutes
	Begin building	15 minutes
	Clean-up	5 minutes
SESSION 2	Introduce session and format for mid-design share-out	10 minutes
	Mid-design share-out	30 minutes
	Partner reflection on feedback during mid-design share-out	10 minutes
SESSION 3	Introduce session and discuss physical testing	5 minutes
	Build, iterate, and test	20 minutes
	Document	10 minutes
SESSION 4	Gallery walk and class reflection	25 minutes

interlocking building blocks, and she wanted everyone to approach the task from a similar starting point. Second, everyday recyclable or craft materials give students a chance to work with materials that vary in texture, weight, absorption, or other qualities. Learning to build with diverse materials is a skill necessary for this and future projects.

Amy sent a letter to families requesting that they send in materials that would typically go in the recycling bin such as yogurt containers and cereal boxes. She wanted to make sure that all families were able to contribute if they wanted to but that the request would not cause undue strain or cause students to feel that they had not contributed. She filled in with other materials that she already had in the classroom such as tape.

Anticipated Conversations and Questions
Amy considered the questions to ask her students and the possible discussions that might occur during the activity

Introduction
- ◆ What makes a chair a chair?
- ◆ What should our chairs be able to do (criteria)?

- ◆ What are constraints?
- ◆ What does it mean to build for a client?
- ◆ What do we think the bears would want and/or need?

Planning
- ◆ Why do we plan?
- ◆ Do you have to build exactly what you plan?

Materials
- ◆ You may need to play with a material for a little before you know exactly how to use it.

Building
- ◆ Things don't always go as planned. How can we deal with failure?

Feedback
- ◆ Ways that you can give useful and appropriate feedback.
- ◆ What do you do with feedback when you get it?

Testing
- ◆ What is the purpose of testing?
- ◆ How can we test the chairs?
- ◆ You'll need to make changes based on how your testing goes.

Scaffolds

For this activity, Amy included a few scaffolds at specific times during the design process. She posted basic information about the activity on the board as a visual reminder. To support planning, she provided the students with sheets to structure their planning process as well as collaboration. Amy customized the planning sheets to meet the needs of a few students with individualized education plans but felt that all her students could benefit from these adjustments. One modification, a checklist, supported executive functioning by helping the students keep track of the different phases of the design process.

Introducing Activity and Materials

Amy brought the students onto a rug to begin the discussion.

Amy: Today we are going to start building chairs. There are many types of chairs. What do you think makes a chair a chair?

The students begin sharing their ideas.

Juan:	A place to sit.
Sophie:	Legs!
Amy:	Let's look at a few pictures of chairs.

Amy found a few pictures of different types of chairs online before the discussion and shared them on the screen.

Amy:	Okay, let's look at these chairs. What do you see?
Marco:	You can sit in them all.
Lea:	They all have a seat.
Arya:	They all have legs.
Amy:	Do they all have the same number of legs?
Malik:	No, one has three legs. The other has four.
Amy:	Is there anything else different between the chairs?

Several students call out that some of the chairs have arms and others do not.

Amy:	So what do we think a chair absolutely needs to have?
Malik:	Legs and a place to sit.
Amy:	What about a back?
Lea:	Yes. No. I don't know. I think a chair without a back is a stool.
Amy:	Okay, for this class let's say that our chairs have to have a seat, legs, and a back. We are going to call those our criteria, or the things that the chair absolutely has to have. Let's think of other criteria. Think about a chair you like.
Gabriella:	It should be comfortable.
Amy:	That makes sense. Okay, let's think about our clients. We'll start with this bear. [Amy shows the students the stuffed bear.] You are going to be building chairs for stuffed animals. That means we need to think about what will work for them. What do you need to think about as you plan and build? How about for this bear?
Marco:	It needs to be the right size.
Celia:	He can't sit up by himself, so it definitely needs to help him.
Amy:	Great. What special considerations will your specific animal need? How will you serve this animal's needs with your chair? Let's think about safety. Would you want to sit in a chair that wobbles?

Gabriella: It should also not break when you sit in it.

Amy: That sounds like a good thing. So we want the chairs to be sturdy. I'll write these on the board under criteria: sturdy, comfortable, legs, a back, and a seat.

I'm going to talk a little bit about constraints, which are limitations you have to work within. One of the limitations is the amount of time you will have. You'll have today to plan and start building and then two or three more sessions after that. Another limitation is materials. You'll all have the same materials to pick from. You don't have to use all of them, but you can't use ones other than those on the materials table.

Amy walks over to the tables and holds up the different materials and names what they are.

Amy: I'm going to give everyone a partner, and then the two of you are going to plan your chairs. You'll get one document to share between the two of you.

Amy projects a copy of the planning document and describes what will go into each section. She stresses that they will be building one chair between the two partners.

Introducing Process and Norms

Once Amy introduced the activity, she used the remaining time to discuss norms and strategies for collaborative group work: "Before we get started, let's talk a little bit about how we are going to work together. We have our usual classroom norms, but can anyone think of others that are good for hands-on group work?" Instead of simply giving students the norms, Amy encouraged the whole class to craft the norms together. The students arrived at the following:

- ◆ Don't take things out of someone else's hands.
- ◆ Don't take apart something someone else built unless you ask.
- ◆ If you don't agree with your partner,
    - – listen to what they are saying and then tell them what you think should happen.
    - – see if you can do part of both the ideas.
    - – make little versions and test both ideas.
- ◆ Nobody owns ideas so it's okay for others to use someone else's idea.

- ◆ If you get really frustrated, it's okay to ask for help.
- ◆ It's okay to fail.

At the end of this conversation, Amy paired the students and had them return to the tables.

Activity in Process

Planning

After the students returned to their tables, Amy reminded them that they would be planning before they built. She handed out a planning sheet to each student and a stuffed animal to each pair. She gave a brief description of each part of the planning document. She reminded them that they are building one chair. Amy asked them to look at their stuffed animals and see if there was anything they needed to think about that was specific to their stuffed animal as they built. Some students mentioned that their animal had a long tail. Others noticed that their stuffed animal was not able to sit up by itself.

Amy told the students they needed first to draw their ideas, but they could stray from those ideas when they started building, and she reminded them to use the drawings to share ideas with their partners. She had two additional reminders about materials: 1) Use the materials on their list first before adding others, and 2) if they do add others, explain how these additional materials contribute to the design. She pointed to the table and said, "These are all the materials we have for this project so please be respectful of others' needs and only take what you need." She hoped that by telling students they could get more materials later that they would not hoard materials at the beginning.

Amy described the two tests: 1) dropping the chair from their ankles to test sturdiness and 2) putting the stuffed animal in the chair without it falling over. She mentioned that groups could add tests depending on their designs. For the final question on the sheet, "What did you notice when you tested your design?" Amy provided the students with a key engineering strategy: "As you test, observe what's working well and what improvements are needed."

As the students planned, Amy circulated and checked in with each group. She asked questions to understand their ideas and to scaffold their executive functioning (e.g., "It looks like you finished your drawing. Have you started thinking about which materials you will use?"). She saw two students, Leena and Ar'Shaye, who were talking about what the seat, which they call the platform, of the chair should be like and manipulating a piece of cardboard as they talked.

Your Name and Your Partner:

Who is your client? _____

Is there anything special you need to think about for your client?

_____

_____

_____

Draw Your Design.

What Materials Will You Use?

What Did You Notice When You Tested Your Design?

What Worked Well?

What Needs To Be Improved?

Leena:	Um, so, what would be like the platform?
Ar'Shaye:	Let's . . .
Leena:	Here, this should be the platform. Ready, let's measure it. Yeah, let's do that. He's a teddy bear so we can squish him. If we put, like, the little arm rests on the side.

Amy noticed that the students were concerned that their bear would not fit into the seat and were thinking about adding arms to their chair. She felt that they were working together effectively and making progress, so she moved on to the next group. This group was having trouble negotiating how to incorporate ideas from each person in the group.

Amy:	How's it going?
Alice:	I want to make a beach chair, and he wants to make a regular chair.
Amy:	Hmm. Can you tell me why you want to make a beach chair?
Alice:	I think he'd want to be comfortable and do something fun, and I thought we could have the back of the chair move.
Amy:	What do you think of that? Why were you thinking of a different kind of chair?
Oscar:	I think the beach would be too hot, and I'm not sure how we'd make the back move and then stay in place.
Alice:	I was thinking we'd have a rod across the back and something that comes out and goes into the bottom.
	Amy looks at Alice's drawing. "Can you tell me what this is?" (pointing to a detail on the drawing).
Alice:	That's the rod. See how it goes into this piece at the bottom.
Ryan:	That might work.
	Ryan turns toward Amy.
Ryan:	Can we look at the materials and see what might work?
Amy:	Sure. Go right ahead.

After discussing with the students, Amy realized that Oscar had hesitated to build the beach chair because he didn't understand Alice's idea about stabilizing the back of the chair.

Many of the groups included a large amount of tape, so Amy reminded them about ways to connect things other than tape. She seldom intervened as the students had lots of good ideas about their chairs. When pairs finished their plan, Amy reviewed and approved them and then suggested they get materials. She made sure that all students made progress but acknowledged that not all students would move to the building phase at the same time.

Building

With their approved plans and building materials in hand, the students began to build their chairs. Again, Amy circulated, observed, asked questions, and encouraged the students to test to make sure the chairs worked for the stuffed animal clients. She saw students measuring their animals to make sure the seats were the correct size and then putting them on the seats to check sizes. She stopped to listen to Leena and Ar'Shaye's conversation discussing how to make something that would support the bear to sit up.

Leena:	Okay, look, I connected these right here. We'll worry about the bottom after. Um . . .
Ar'Shaye:	So let's try to make him sit up straight, 'cause he's just gonna keep doing this [demonstrates the bear falling over].
Leena:	Okay yeah, that's true. So, we need something like this. There we go! Um, just stack more on top.
Ar'Shaye:	I think that's too long.
Leena:	I didn't even notice that. Yeah that one's way too long. Ugh, stick together! There we go.
Ar'Shaye:	Oh . . .
Ar'Shaye:	Okay, we got him to sit up. I know what you're talking about. Like a high chair kind of connecting thing.
Leena:	Yeah.
Ar'Shaye:	Like Boop! [attaches a connecting piece]
Leena:	Yeah, but it needs to be a little higher, so his thick legs could fit through.
Ar'Shaye:	[gasps] Ooh!
	Something does not fit together like Ar'Shaye thought it would.
Leena:	Yeah, but like through here. It won't fit.
	Leena takes off the pieces that Ar'Shaye just added.
Ar'Shaye:	You just took apart—

At this point, Amy walked up to the pair.

Amy:	Can you guys tell me about your idea?
Leena:	Um, so we really just did the backrest.
Ar'Shaye:	places the bear in the chair.
Leena:	Um, and maybe we're gonna need to make the bottom a little wider [takes the bear out of the chair]. But then, we like, then we are gonna make this part higher. And then we're gonna

put something like this, so his fit, so his legs can fit through. And then probably make something like a seatbelt.

Amy: Okay. I like the way you are testing as you go, putting him in the seat to make sure the size is right and will support him.

The two students continued to build, working on making the seat wider.

Amy next saw a pair of students who seemed to be struggling to attach the legs of their chair.

Amy: How's it going?

Naya: Our chair is okay, but when we put the bear in it, the legs [paper cups attached with a piece of tape] fall off.

Amy: The legs fall off? Why do you think that is happening?

Sean: The bear weighs too much?

Amy: Why do you think it's because the bear weight too much?

Sean: Well, when we. . . . Well, watch.

Sean puts the bear on the chair, and one of the legs splays out, and then the seat of the chair slides to the table.

Amy: I see what you mean. What do you think you can change?

Naya: I feel like they should work.

Amy: How are you attaching the legs?

Naya: We have a piece of tape, but maybe it's not enough.

Amy: Not enough?

Naya: Not enough tape or not enough support for the leg, so it stays.

Sean: Can we have more tape?

Amy: Of course, but can you think of another way you could attach it besides tape?

Sean: I don't think glue because the bottom of the cup has a ridge. Maybe we could use one of those metal things that has legs.

Amy: That has legs?

Sean walks to the materials table and grabs a metal brad.

Sean: This.

Amy: Ah. Naya, what do you think of that idea?

Naya: That could work. I like that once you put it where it should go, it won't slide.

Amy: Okay, give it a try and test it with the bear again. Good problem solving.

As you can see with this last conversation, Amy made sure that when students struggled, she did not tell them how to fix the issue. Instead, she asked questions to guide them to solve the problem themselves. Her questions were either open ended or echoed the students' responses, encouraging them to expand their responses rather than simply deliver a specific answer.

The students continued to work for another few minutes before the period ended. Amy reminded them that they had a few more days to work and that nobody had finished yet. She asked them to record their next steps in their engineering journals. After the students had cleaned up, Amy asked them to reflect on their experience so far. She asked the students to share what was going well and where they were having difficulty. Encouraging the students to share ideas supported her goal of building collaborative problem-solving skills. Amy started the next engineering session by reminding students to test as they go and to check their engineering journals to remind them of where to start. She gave them ten minutes to build before a mid-design share-out.

Peer Reviews

In addition to physical testing, peer reviews support students in sharing their ideas and get feedback on their designs. Share-outs can happen at various points during the design process. Teachers can facilitate these reviews with the whole class, with individual groups, or between several groups. We've found it more beneficial for students to share their designs before completion rather than adhering to the common practice of final presentations. In fact, share-outs that occur midway through the activity more closely reflect the process that professional engineers use. Students can make changes and fix problems based on suggestions from peers. The format of a mid-design review can involve sharing in front of the entire class, in small groups, or a combination of both.

Amy began the second session by introducing the peer design review to gather information used to make improvements on designs:

You've been physically testing your chairs which gives you one type of feedback, but today we are going to get peer feedback. Feedback from others is helpful because they may be able to think of something to solve a problem you are having or address something that you haven't thought of yet. Hearing from other people who are working on similar things or having similar problems may benefit you because maybe they solved a problem you are having. So, I want you all to not only talk about what is going well for you, but share things you aren't sure about, things that are not working yet, and even things that you have tried that have not worked at all.

Amy hoped that encouraging students to share uncertainties and failures would make them more willing to talk about problems they faced.

In addition, Amy set expectations for both parts of the share-out, the idea presentations and the feedback. Amy gave an example of a format that they could use: "If you aren't sure how to get started, you can think about these three questions."

1) What was successful about my design?
2) What isn't working about my design?
3) What will I change to make the design better?

Also, this isn't a long presentation. I'm thinking that each group's review will take three or four minutes and that you will not be talking the whole time, but part of the time people will be giving you suggestions and asking questions.

Since the students hadn't performed peer reviews before, Amy talked to them about giving and getting feedback:

After a group has shared their design ideas, they'll ask for comments or questions. If you are in the audience, you can point out something that you like about their design or you can ask a question if you have something you are wondering about. Maybe you have a suggestion for improvement based on something that you did and that you think will help them. Keep in mind that suggestions should be kind, be specific, and be helpful (Berger et al., 2016). The reason you are talking to them is because you want to help them. If you are presenting and getting suggestions, you can thank the person who is giving it. It's not expected that you will incorporate all the suggestions, but just that you will consider their ideas.

Amy felt that the students understood but decided to model what it looked like to present ideas, which she did by using one of the student's chairs and pretending she had made it: "I made this chair and think it's pretty sturdy. I wish it had arms but am not sure how I would add them. And it doesn't really fit me. Does anyone have any ideas?" The students giggled and then started to raise their hands.

Aiya: You could make the seat bigger.
Amy: That could work. What do you think I could use?
Aiya: Maybe use a bigger piece of wood and just put it right on top.
Oscar: What if you tie a dowel rod to the back and one of the legs?
Amy: You mean for the arms?
Oscar: Yes, the arms.
Amy: I'll have to think about that. I'm not sure I could make them so
        I could put weight on them, but I would like to have arms. I'm
        going to point out that I heard what you all said and responded
        to your suggestions, but I didn't say that I am definitely doing

any of them. It's okay to say that you are going to think about it when you start working again. Let's switch so now I am giving feedback. Would someone be willing to share their chair?

Two students raised their hands and went to the front of the room: "This is our chair. It fits the bear and is mostly sturdy, but the back sometimes moves around." Amy said,

Okay, I'm going to try to be kind, specific, and helpful. I really like how your chair has a space in the back for your alligator's tail. I see your back is attached at the very bottom. I'm wondering if you attach it in more places, maybe one more spot on either side that goes from the back to the seat if that will keep the back from moving.

The class discussed Amy's comments before starting. She reminded them to refer to the poster for help with the discussion. Although helpful for *all* students, the poster, Figure 7.2, was particularly useful for a few students who benefited from visual cues and needed more processing time.

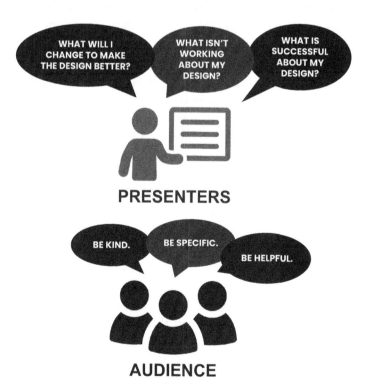

Figure 7.2 Poster content guiding students as presenters and audience members.

Each group spent a few minutes presenting their design. There were a few moments where students struggled with the process a bit, but overall, the first design review worked well. Amy believed that with practice, students would start initiating and owning the conversations. After the share-out, she told the students to write down any ideas they had heard and liked in their engineering journals. reminded them to use these ideas when they started building in their next session.

Physical Testing

At the beginning of the third session, Amy reminded students that it was the final day of building and that they should check their engineering journals before beginning. All students had tested their chairs with the stuffed animals, but not all groups had conducted the drop test. Although she reminded students they needed to do this test, she did not pressure anyone into doing it, recognizing that most students were still working on the sturdiness of their chairs. She decided to have a brief conversation about physical testing.

Amy:	Everyone has been testing their chairs with their stuffed animals to make sure they fit. Yesterday you got one kind of feedback from your peers. Most of you have not done the drop test though. Do you think you want to do the drop test at the very end of building? Why or why not?
Omar:	Well, if you wait until the end, it might break and then you wouldn't have time to fix it.
Aiya:	Yeah, but if you drop it before you are done and it really breaks, then you might not have time to fix it in time to share it.
Amy:	Both are good arguments, but let me ask, if you buy a chair, do you want to sit on it if nobody has tested it to see how sturdy it is? Or think of a bridge before the first car goes across. Do you want to be that first car?
	Many students giggle.

Amy suggested that groups bring their chairs onto the rug since the rug might be a safer place to test the chairs than the hard floor. As the students built, Amy checked in with individual groups to make sure they knew where to start. A few pairs walked up to drop their chairs from their ankles. Most of the chairs detached in a minor way. As the students dropped their chairs, Amy asked them what was not working about their design and what needed to change. When more than one group tested at the same time, she encouraged group conversations, so students could analyze and give feedback to each other. Amy happily noticed that students used the peer feedback skills they had learned in the last session. She kept the testing low-stakes and fun so students could see that it was okay if their chair was not 100% sturdy.

Amy gave the students a five-minute warning to the end of building time before students returned to their seats. She told them to document what they had been doing. She wrote some questions on the board and asked them to answer them in the engineering journal. They did this until the end of class.

Final Session

By the end of the last class, most students had completed their chairs. Amy gave those students who had not finished another ten minutes to complete their chairs. The other students put finishing touches on their chairs and worked on the documentation they had started last time. After ten minutes she called the students to the rug and asked them to bring their chairs. The students shared a special feature of their chair or something that they liked about it.

Students were excited to share their chairs. See Figure 7.3 for sample chairs. Some students added a footrest. One had a tail rest. The students who had discussed the beach chair made one with a reclining back. After everyone shared, the students put each of their stuffed animals in their chair and then looked at all the other chairs. Next, she told students to take the stuffed animals out of the chairs to do some "quality control" and a safety check. The students became excited because they knew they would get to drop their chairs. Amy reminded them that it's okay if they don't stay together. The students stood up, and on the count of three, they dropped the chairs from their ankles. Everyone laughed.

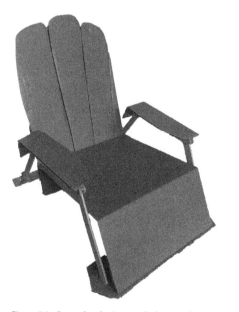

Figure 7.3 Sample chairs made by students.

Finally, Amy asked the students what they thought about the activity. Most of the students said it was fun and that they liked building. She then asked if it was difficult to come up with all the ideas. One student said that at first it was hard because they could do anything, but then it got easier. Amy then asked the students if it was hard when their chairs didn't work in ways they had planned. Some students nodded their heads. James shared that he got really frustrated.

James:	The first time we did the drop test because the back came off. I didn't want to do it anymore.
Amy:	What changed your mind?
James:	My partner didn't seem upset, so I thought I would work a little more and see.
Amy:	Are you glad that you did?
James:	Yeah, it was more fun after that.
Amy:	I'm glad you continued. I think everyone had a moment when they got frustrated. Even though engineering is fun, sometimes it can get frustrating. Do others think that?
	Some kids nod their heads.
Amy:	We'll do some more engineering this year. I'm sure there will be more frustration, but I think it will mostly be fun, and I think you all are going to make some amazing things.

Amy and her class used this as a launching activity for engineering in the classroom and did several other design challenges throughout the year. Amy made sure that each activity gave students the opportunity to engage in different engineering practices.

This chapter detailed one introductory experience. The teacher chose the bear chair activity based on what she felt her students were capable of doing. She selected subsequent activities that built off these initial skills and introduced new ones to learn and practice. Although teachers might plan a sequence of activities for the year, it's important to be flexible, build on students' strengths, and provide opportunities for them to work on new skills.

If students need more experience with foundational building or collaboration skills, we recommend implementing an additional introductory activity prior to one like Chair for a Bear. Sometimes students need several introductory activities to practice these new engineering skills. The next chapter presents several introductory activities that can act as skill and knowledge builders and introduce engineering and related skills and classroom norms.

Reference

Berger, R., Woodfin, L, & Vilen, A. (2016). *Learning that lasts: Challenging, engaging, and empowering students with deeper instruction.* San Francisco, CA: Jossey-Bass.

8

Getting Started With Engineering
Sample Introductory Activities

In the last chapter, focusing on the Chair for a Bear activity, the students worked their way through the EDP. In this chapter, each activity highlights different phases of the process and helps students build foundational skills. In general, introductory activities should:

- provide a context for conversations about engineering.
- provide students with a common experience upon which to base discussions.
- help establish classroom culture and norms.
- provide students with a low-stakes experience.
- allow for flexibility of implementation and diversity of solutions.

Most of these activities are best suited for pairs of students. In pairs, students can work on co-design skills building. For these simpler, introductory activities, more than two students present several disadvantages. First, there is usually not enough work for more than two students. Second, some students do not get to put their hands on the project. Third, additional group members can create a more complicated dynamic when students are just learning to collaborate; students spend more time negotiating ideas rather than building. In the next few pages, we'll present activities highlighting both the engineering learning as well as the social and emotional learning that typically occurs during these activities.

We chose the following activities because they meet the criteria for introductory activities and we have seen them successfully implemented with

DOI: 10.4324/9781003378174-8

students. We do not anticipate that a class would do all the activities; rather, we anticipate that teachers will pick the ones that will meet their own classroom goals and be most appropriate and interesting for the students. Lesson plans for the activities are in the appendix.

Activity 1 – Focus on Design Criteria: Product Comparison

Learning Objectives
Students will:

- ◆ practice collaborating with a partner.
- ◆ better understand the properties of materials.
- ◆ gain experience testing.

In this activity, students compare different versions of the same product to understand that there is not always one perfect solution or design. For example, they will look at four different pens and think about the pros and cons of each type of pen. In addition to weighing the pros and cons of a design, students practice coming to a consensus when negotiating their ideas. Students, especially younger ones, often think there is one correct answer or one best design. They focus on finding the perfect design to address a problem. They do not consider the pros and cons of different design ideas, the stakeholders, the end user, and many other design elements. This activity will engage all students more readily if they are working with a familiar item.

The first step is to give each student a blank product comparison table (see Appendix G). Discussing the items in their small groups of three to four students, they complete this table. Figure 8.1 details the EDP skills that are highlighted in this activity.

However, before students begin discussing their own items, instructors should model the activity with the whole class using an item they will not use. Why is modeling important? Modeling the activity helps students develop vocabulary related to engineering such as constraints and criteria, as well as vocabulary related to collaboration and negotiation.

We share an example from a fifth-grade class where the students must select the best water bottle from five different choices. The teacher began by modeling the activity using five different pens to compare. As a class, the students discussed which characteristics were important when choosing a pen. They chose cost, fluidity of ink, attractiveness, grip comfort, and engagement of the point (click, cap, or twist). Then, through discussion they decided that

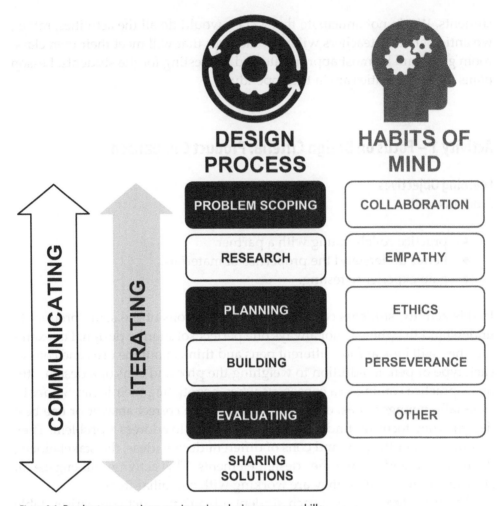

DESIGN PROCESS

HABITS OF MIND

COMMUNICATING

ITERATING

PROBLEM SCOPING	COLLABORATION
RESEARCH	EMPATHY
PLANNING	ETHICS
BUILDING	PERSEVERANCE
EVALUATING	OTHER
SHARING SOLUTIONS	

Figure 8.1 Product comparison engineering design process skills.

the best pen depended on several factors including who and where the user is. Here is a short excerpt of that discussion.

Johnny: If you are a teacher and you lend your pen to your students, you won't want to buy expensive pens because the students will take them. By accident.

Astrid: But if you want to make sure you have a nice pen, you wouldn't give that one to the students so you could choose one that is nicer.

Paul: I would be okay spending a little more (as a student) on a pen because I keep it in my backpack and nobody else would use it. So I wouldn't lose it.

Astrid: Right, it just depends.

Once this discussion wrapped up, the teacher introduced the water bottles and split the class into groups of four, gave them the product comparison worksheet, and asked them to do the same activity. Additionally, the teacher told them that each student needed to pick the bottle that was best suited to him or her personally and then convince the class of their choice. Students identified characteristics such as cost, environmental-friendliness, size, weight, ease of use, and way to drink the water (straw, screw-off top, etc.). Again, they deliberated about which characteristics were best for different users. For example, a hiker might want something lightweight but large enough to hold enough water for a hike. A teacher sitting in the same room all day would want something large enough to last since time to fill up is limited. Each group presented their choice and rationale to the class. An example of one group's completed work is in Figure 8.2.

We've done this with younger groups as well. In second grade, students were asked to pick the best folder for their writing workshop; in this class, the teacher said she would buy whichever folder the class agreed to use the rest of the year. They considered durability, attractiveness, cost, environmental impact, and number of pockets. After each group picked a folder, they wrote a letter to the teacher explaining which folder they had picked and why they had picked the folder. First-graders considered pencils for kindergarteners; they took this very seriously because they had just completed kindergarten. In each of these cases, the teachers wanted the students to realize that there

Product Comparison Water Bottles

Product	Criteria 1 Cost	Criteria 2 Size	Criteria 3 Environment-impact	Criteria 4 Lid	Criteria 5 Carrying Comfort	Notes Who would this be good for?
Disposable	99 cents	8 oz	Very bad	Screw cap, easy to loose, but you drink it quickly	average	Good if you are really thirsty and don't have a bottle
Insulated	$20	24 oz	Medium – reusable, but plastic	Pop top	Light	Sports player, hiker
Metal	$32.00	24 oz	Good	Cap is not attached, screws off, could loose it	Sort of heavy, but has a strap to carry it	Someone at a desk
Plastic	$15.00	30 oz.	Medium – reusable, but plastic	Cap attached, straw	Light, good handle	Someone who walks around a lot

Figure 8.2 Completed water bottle product comparison worksheet.

are multiple solutions and that the appropriate solution is usually tied to the context and user.

Since this activity requires negotiation and collaboration, students practice skills in building relationships and social awareness. Some students may need more support than others working in a group who must come to a consensus. Providing students with clear expectations such as "all students deserve to be heard" as well as offering strategies for resolving group conflicts can support participation among all group members.

Activity 2 – Focus on Building: Pencil Holder

Using recyclable and craft materials, students will design something to hold eight to twelve pencils or pens on their desk or table. (See Appendix H for pencil holder lesson plan.)

Learning Objectives
Students will:

- ◆ practice collaborating with a partner.
- ◆ understand the properties of materials.
- ◆ gain experience testing.
- ◆ understand constraints and criteria.

This is a quick activity to introduce students to the EDP with an option to focus on specific phases of the process. Since most students are familiar with pencils holders, the activity ensures that students of varying levels of building experience can participate. Also, although many people have similar ideas of what a pencil holder is, this activity offers the opportunity for a diversity of solutions. In the classes we have worked with, we have seen pencil keepers with lids as well as containers that hold pencils, erasers, scissors, and other objects. Another group used wire and built a holder that hung from their desks. It is possible to create more variety if students have different items or if they work on different locations such as their desks or tables.

Discussing Constraints and Criteria
Teachers can use this activity to introduce the concept of constraints and criteria. Constraints are limitations or restrictions on the project. Criteria are standards against which their designs should be compared to show that the designs work and meet users' needs. With the whole class, have students discuss possible constraints and criteria for the project. Possible constraints

and criteria are outlined in Table 8.1, and Figure 8.3 highlights which EDP skills are emphasized during this process. Use these conversations to model and give explicit instructions on how to engage in productive and respectful conversations, especially when disagreements occur.

Table 8.1 Possible Criteria and Constraints for a Pencil Holder

Possible Criteria	Possible Constraints
• Sturdy • Large enough to hold 8-10 items • Must fit in a specific location	• Only uses materials in the classroom • Must be completed in 30 minutes

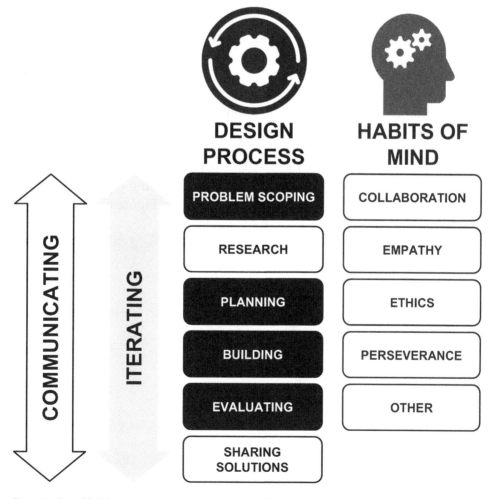

Figure 8.3 Pencil holder engineering design process skills.

Planning

Depending on your goals, planning for this project can be a basic sketch on a blank sheet of paper or a longer planning document. For students who need more executive functioning support, planning sheets can be scaffolded. For example, open responses may be fitting for some students while others may need sentence starters or fill-in-the-blank responses. Other students might benefit from a checklist of the student-developed list of constraints and criteria. The planning sheet can also help facilitate communication between partners since it can provide a tangible focus when students are discussing ideas.

Physical Testing

Testing for this activity is very straightforward given the constraints of sturdiness and function. As they build, encourage students to test their designs by putting items inside to see if they fit and if the holder stays together. Talk to students about how the purpose of testing is to show where the design is doing well and where a change would improve the design.

Feedback Session

Facilitating a mid-design share-out soon after students begin building has two advantages: A mid-design share-out contributes to students' understanding of how to give and receive feedback and helps build a community of collaboration. In this activity, groups can test each other's designs by placing pencils in them. Groups offer feedback to each other based on the testing results and suggestions that come up as they are testing and talking to the designers. Examples of student work can be seen in Figure 8.4. Examples of different feedback structures are included in Chapter 11.

Sample Solutions

Figure 8.4 Sample pencil holders.

 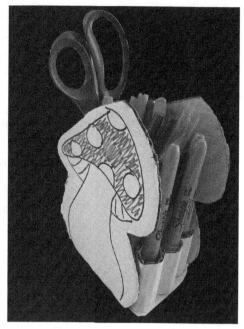

Figure 8.4 (Continued)

Activity 3 – Focus on Testing and Iteration: Wind Tube

Students will build something that hovers in a 4' plastic tube around the middle for three to ten seconds. It can move around the middle but can't go out the top or fall to the bottom. See Appendices I and J for wind tube lesson plan and building directions.

Learning Objectives
Students will:

◆ gain experience testing and iterating.
◆ understand constraints and criteria.
◆ practice effective collaboration.
◆ practice managing frustration productively.

During this activity, students quickly build, test, and then iterate on their designs so they can build multiple versions. The teacher provides the constraints and criteria as outlined in Table 8.2. Building multiple versions provides an opportunity for students to discuss the role of testing and iteration as well as strategies for effective collaboration with their peers. In addition, while most students enjoy the rapid cycle of testing and iteration, they may become frustrated because their initial designs will probably fail. It is helpful to remind students that failure is an expected and integral part of the design process. Teachers can open a dialogue on failure and talk about strategies to deal with this frustration. It's part of the process.

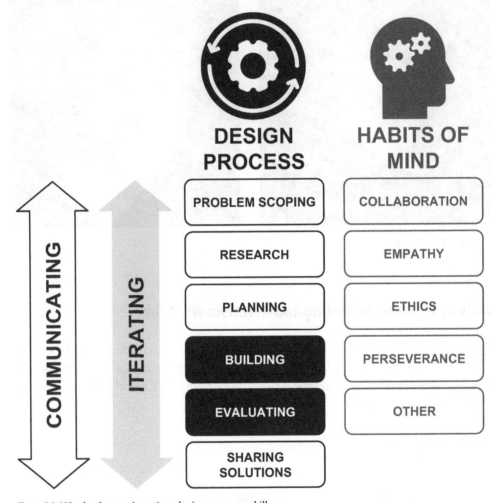

Figure 8.5 Wind tube engineering design process skills.

Table 8.2 Possible Criteria and Constraints for the Wind Tube Activity

Possible Criteria	Possible Constraints
• Hovers for 3–10 seconds between the top and middle bands (or top and bottom) • Fits comfortably within the tube	• Only uses materials available in the classroom • Must secure small items, paper clips and coins for safety

Planning

Formal planning is not necessary for this activity. With their partners, students will touch and manipulate the materials as they figure out what to build. Handling the materials is especially beneficial to students who lack much experience with these resources.

Testing

Encourage students to test numerous times. While students are testing, facilitate impromptu conversations that are relevant to each group's design and ideas. Try to get an understanding of the thinking behind their designs. While students are testing their designs, make it a low-stakes situation and present it as a fun way to get feedback and lower the pressure around designs being successful. In the following conversation, note how the teacher deals with the students' design when it flies out of the tube.

Teacher: Okay Julia and Omar, your last design sank to the bottom right away. What did you change?

Julia: We took away the pennies.

Teacher: Interesting. Can you tell me why you chose to remove all the pennies?

Omar: We thought if it was lighter, it wouldn't sink like last time.

Teacher: That makes sense. Ready to put it in the wind tube?

Julia places their design a few inches inside the tube and removes her hand, and it immediately flies over their heads. The teacher giggles a little.

Teacher: Oh my gosh! What do you think?

Julia: That was crazy.

Omar: I guess we should have left some of the pennies.

Julia: Yeah, let's add a few back.

Teacher: It was still pretty cool to watch it fly out. Luckily, we still have twenty minutes for you to work on your design.

Julia and Omar go back to their desks.

For students who are getting frustrated when their designs do not work the first time, remind them of the conversation about dealing with frustration at the beginning of the activity.

Mid-Design Feedback Session

Craft the mid-design feedback session based on observations made during the activity. A discussion on frustration is useful if students are struggling with perceived design failures. On the other hand, students enjoy sharing success with their materials or combinations of materials. Prompt students to share tips and tricks when building, as well as ways to deal with constraints. Finally, the mid-design feedback session is an opportune time to reflect on group and partner dynamics as well as discuss collaboration within the class community.

Final Discussion

As part of the final group discussion, address any issues around failure, the benefits of quick prototyping, and the role of testing. Possible prompts include the following:

- ◆ How many versions did you make?
- ◆ How did you feel when your design didn't work?
- ◆ How did you decide what changes to make to your design?
- ◆ Did you use input from other groups to make changes?

Activity 4 – Building for a Client: Backpack for a Stuffed Animal

Students will build a backpack for a client, a stuffed animal, to help the stuffed animals carry items.

Students will:

- ◆ outline design constraints and criteria for a specific client.
- ◆ develop a solution based on identified constraints and criteria of a specific client.

This activity introduces two engineering practices: 1) problem scoping and 2) defining constraints and criteria to meet clients' needs; Figure 8.6 shows the EDP skills that are highlighted in this stage. In this case, even though the clients—stuffed animals—are not real, they come with information to inform designs. For example, since each stuffed animal will be of a different size and shape, each pair of students will customize their carrier for their assigned stuffed animal. Examples of student solutions are seen in Figure 8.7. (See Appendix K for Backpack for a Stuffed Animal lesson plan.)

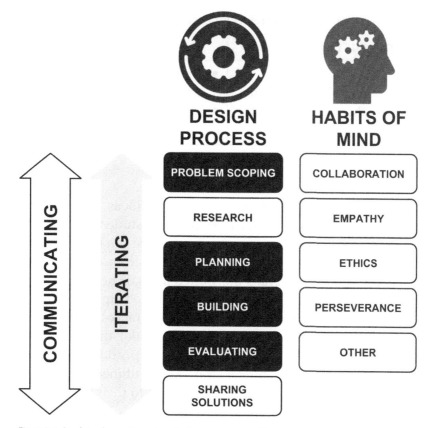

Figure 8.6 Backpack engineering design process skills.

Figure 8.7 Student sample backpack solutions.

Table 8.3 Possible Criteria and Constraints for Backpack Activity

Possible Criteria	Possible Constraints
• Sturdy • Large enough to hold 2–3 items • Must fit on the stuffed animal • Removable	• Only use materials in the classroom • Must be completed in x minutes

Activity Framing

This activity involves brainstorming and sharing ideas about the materials and the clients, the stuffed animals. First, have the students brainstorm ways that class materials such as pencils, crayons, or tape can be carried; students can share ways that they bring materials to and from school. Next, introduce the clients and the materials the stuffed animals need to carry around. Remind students they will be building something to help the stuffed animals carry these items. Discuss the similarities and differences between the different stuffed animals, and encourage students to tailor their solutions to the stuffed animals' shapes, size, and needs. As a group, address the constraints and criteria. Possible criteria and constraints are outlined in Table 8.3. Each group will probably add items to the list specific to their individual stuffed animals.

Planning

Have each pair of students manipulate the stuffed animal and the materials. This hands-on time allows them to explore design constraints imposed by the animal's shape (size, tail, etc.) and the properties of the materials. Have students complete the planning sheets (Appendix A) as a guide to launch their exploration.

Testing

Encourage students to test as they go. They should test for the backpack's fit on the stuffed animal and its ability to hold materials. Students can test either at a class central testing station that has items for the backpack or at their individual workstations with their own materials. Support testing with questions such as the following:

◆ Does the backpack fit onto the animal?
◆ How do you take it off and on?
◆ Do all the items fit into the backpack?

Design Shares

At a mid-design share-out, students can talk about what they are building, problems to figure out, and building tips. During a final share-out, they can show how their design met their client's needs and how they addressed the constraints and criteria. Teachers could use the following as possible prompts for design shares:

- ◆ How did you deal with constraints and criteria as you were building? What was easy and what was challenging?
- ◆ Tell me how you think your design would be different if you did not have a client?
- ◆ What are you unsure about in your design that others might be able to offer suggestions?

Activity 5 – Thinking About Systems: Create a System to Lift a Weight Onto a Chair

To solve this challenge, students will create a system to lift a weight such as a block or a bag of coins onto a chair; students will not touch the weight directly when lifting it.

Learning Objectives

Students will build collaboration skills as they think about the properties of materials and how they interact in a system and practice consensus building when building a system. In this activity, students build a simple machine to lift a weight. To do this, students create something that has several components. Students often make pulley systems or other devices that can lift objects. Some teachers have specifically told their students that they must use a simple machine and that they must be able to move the weight without touching it directly or indirectly with an implement. Possible design constraints and criteria are outlined in Table 8.4. During the introduction, talk to students about dividing the work and communicating with their partners. Since this challenge involves several components, emphasize the importance of communication, planning, and clear division of work. Figure 8.8 details the EDP skills that students may use. Example student solutions can be seen in Figure 8.9. (See Appendix L for the lesson plan to create a system to lift a weight.)

Table 8.4 Possible Criteria and Constraints for Crane Activity

Possible Criteria	Possible Constraints
• Must lift weights • Base must not be held while the weights are being lifted	• Must only use classroom materials • Each group can only use 1' of tape

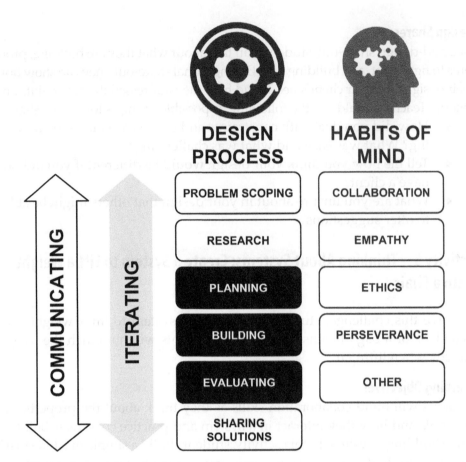

Figure 8.8 Crane engineering design process skills.

Figure 8.9 Student sample crane solutions.

Planning

While students plan, have them identify the different components that they will need to build such as a pulley, pillars that holds the pulley, and a connector for the bucket. Encourage the students to divide the labor, deciding who does which part and how their parts fit together.

Testing

A designated testing station is not necessary since students have access to their materials as they build. Most students will simply use any available table or chair and then their weight.

Design Share

Mid-design and final share-outs can focus on the different systems and individual components. During a mid-design share-out, students might share tips as well as present parts that are not working well to get ideas from their classmates. In addition, they might check in with students on the process of dividing tasks and their partner or group collaboration.

Possible Discussions

- ◆ How did other groups' ideas help you or not?
- ◆ How did you manage dividing the tasks and deciding who would do which one?
- ◆ What challenged you most in this activity? Why?

Activity 6 – Materials Exploration for Students: Build a House

Students will build a house that is able to withstand simulated wind and rain. Houses are tested with a hair dryer and spray from a water bottle. By building homes for different regions of the county or world, students connect to a social studies lesson.

Learning Objectives

Students will:

- ◆ gain experience connecting different materials.
- ◆ better understand properties of materials.
- ◆ practice collaboration, negotiation and idea sharing.

Introduction

To introduce the activity, present images of houses to talk about why they are designed in a specific way. For example, in New England, most houses have a pitched roof rather than a flat roof so that high volumes of snow do not rest on the roofs causing them to collapse. Given the criteria of sturdiness and water-proofness, discuss the properties of different materials. Students will need to understand how to attach materials to each other so they stay together.

You may choose to give all students access to the same materials or assign specific materials to different pairs. At the end of the activity, each group can present an overview of building tips and properties of each material. When students work with different materials and share ideas, they create a culture of shared knowledge. The engineering design skills for this activity are outlined in Figure 8.10. (See Appendix M for the Build a House lesson plan.)

Some teachers have extended this activity by having students write a blurb about the homes they built as part of a real estate listing. Teachers who choose that direction should share some required criteria and constraints and facilitate a discussion to see if students have other criteria and constraints to include. Possible constraints are outlined in Table 8.5.

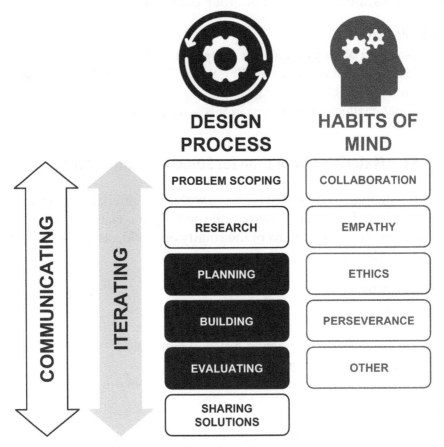

Figure 8.10 House-building engineering design process skills.

Table 8.5 Possible Criteria and Constraints for House Activity

Possible Criteria	Possible Constraints
• Sturdy enough to withstand the wind for 15 seconds • Each side must be between 12–15" • Must have at least one door and two windows	• Only uses classroom materials • Must be completed in x minutes

Planning

Students will need to manipulate materials as they plan. Using a simple planning sheet, they can note the use and purpose of each material in the design.

Building

Give students a piece of cardboard to use as a base for the houses. Walk around checking in on students as they build.

Testing

A testing station with a hair dryer and spray bottle will encourage students to test as they build.

Sharing

During a mid-design share-out, have students offer building tips to each other, which is especially useful if students are working with different materials. Students can report on the properties of the materials and what's working and what's not. During a final share-out, students can show how their houses work during a rainstorm and a windstorm. One student solution can be seen in Figure 8.11.

Possible Discussion Prompts for Share-Outs

- ◆ Were some materials harder or easier to work with than you anticipated? Why?
- ◆ What were the pro and cons of different materials?
- ◆ Which materials were best suited for making sturdy structures?
- ◆ What building techniques did you use? How did you attach materials to each other? Which materials were best for connecting?
- ◆ What did you see among your peers that was helpful?

We've shared several activities that are effective launching points for engineering in the classroom. The activities vary, so teachers can select ones that meet

Figure 8.11 Sample student house solution.

the needs, interests, and experiences of their students. Using a string of short activities is useful for teachers without a lot of time to devote to engineering. Many teachers prefer to use these activities to help their students to gain foundational engineering skills before moving to more complex activities.

The next section of the book details ways to facilitate activities as well as resources for teachers to design their own activities. Using existing activities is beneficial for teachers with limited experience doing engineering in the classroom. On the other hand, designing original activities allows customization to meet the classes' specific needs, especially when integrating engineering with other disciplines. The next section of the book also addresses practical logistics such as material selection, documentation, and assessment.

9

Writing and Drawing to Support Engineering Thinking

In Chapters 9 and 10, we look beyond supporting students in creating functional designs to other aspects of learning activities that support engineering thinking. In this chapter, the focus is on annotations such as writing, drawing, photographs, and combinations of these such as annotating a photo. Annotations are meant to provide a reader or viewer with an enhanced understanding. The previous chapters have included examples of ways both students and instructors use writing, drawing, and photos; in this chapter, we consider these options and discuss the rationale for choosing one over the other or combinations. In Chapter 10, we focus on supporting whole-class engineering discussions.

Documentation is useful to designers in many disciplines, not just engineering. First, it simply helps the creator remember what they have designed, and second, a visual representation can highlight aspects of a design that might have been missed. In addition, these external representations can make thinking visible so others can interact with the ideas. Finally, documentation helps instructors gain insight into how students understand a task and their progress with that task. We advocate sharing the purpose of documentation with students. Remind them that writing, drawing, and taking photographs improve a design by building knowledge and facilitating interaction with the design.

Students will often document their work while they are talking through the design with a partner or in a small group. After handling the materials, students discuss and then record their ideas as references while working on the project. Or instead of writing design ideas, some students opt to sketch or

DOI: 10.4324/9781003378174-9

draw and then explain their drawings to their group. And in other instances, students take individual notes and then share them with their partner, group, or whole class.

As always, we emphasize that the goal of drawing, writing, and taking photos is to help students or teachers document and share ideas. We organize this chapter by the three phases of engineering design: defining, iterating (what the Next Generation Science Standards call optimizing), and sharing. Writing, drawing, and taking pictures occur in all three phases, but they serve a different purpose in each phase.

Defining Phase

In the defining phase, the goal is to understand the problem and think about possible solutions. Defining includes problem scoping and brainstorming. This phase may require looking at previous or similar solutions and/or learning about a client, user, or context. Students may brainstorm individually or in groups to generate ideas in written lists, descriptions, drawings, or collections of images. Many teachers lead whole-class discussions to create a list of criteria and constraints. Some students sketch physical ideas at this stage before building them. To evaluate designs, some students also draft testing procedures that include sketches, text of steps, and a written list of materials needed. Different types of annotation can be used to support the goals of the defining phase. Table 9.1 outlines the different annotation options to support these three goals.

Table 9.1 Types of Annotation to Support Three Potential Goals in the Defining Phase

Brainstorm Many Ideas	Define the Problem and Solution	Make Progress on a Few Ideas
• List possible solutions. • Collect pictures of existing similar problems or solutions.	• Write a list of criteria and constraints. • Write or draw a plan to evaluate design. • Write a description of client or user needs or preferences.	• Sketch ideas for designs that will be built (maybe with labels). • List potential materials.

When initiating the defining phase, teachers choose whether to have students work in small groups or stay together as a whole class. For example, if the design problem is open-ended with no predetermined materials, brainstorming the materials list as a whole group can boost innovation, creativity and collaborative development of ideas. On the other hand, if there is a limited set of materials, each group can write down which and how much of each material they need to ensure that there is enough for the class.

In a hand-pollinator task inspired by the Engineering is Elementary (EiE) curriculum unit (Museum of Science, Boston, 2015), a fourth-grade teacher created an anchor chart including 1) a summary of how pollen travels by bees between flowers, which students described after a read-aloud, and (2) a list of design needs determined by the students, initial small group brainstorming (see Figure 9.1).

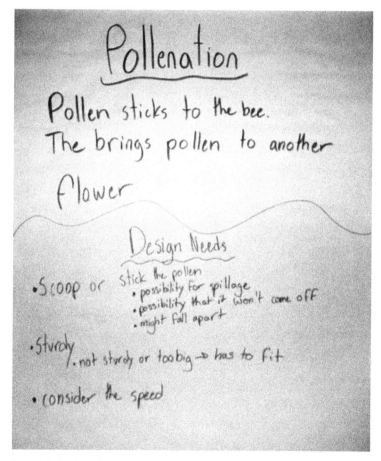

Figure 9.1 Anchor chart for hand-pollinator design task based on whole-class discussion.

In this same lesson, the teacher gave students printed handouts to sketch their design ideas and list the needed materials. To ensure multiple design ideas, the teacher designed the worksheet with space for four separate designs the children could choose from, as seen in Figure 9.2. Although these students worked in groups of three, each student had a worksheet to draw their own design idea.

Name: ███████████████   Date: ███████

Hand Pollinators: Imagine, Improve, and Reflect

Imagine

Brainstorm ideas for your hand pollinators in the table below. Make sure you list the materials that you'll need below your design. Decide which design you think will work best.

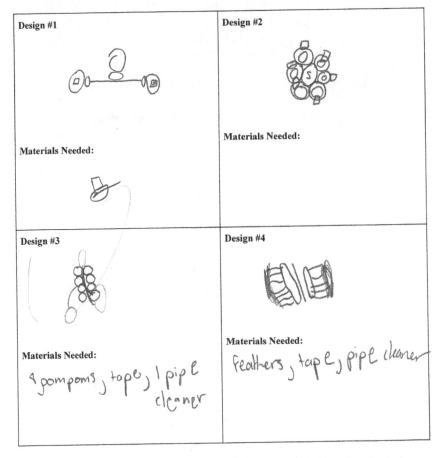

Figure 9.2 Hand-pollinator idea generation worksheet completed by a fourth-grader.

Iterating Phase

In the iteration phase, the goal is to create, test, and improve designs, which involves figuring out what is working or not working about a design and why.

One important part of the iteration phase is receiving and interpreting feedback from physical tests. Documentation supports students in evaluating their design iterations. If there are more than two trials, it is challenging to remember the results of each iteration. In some cases, it's enough to draw a quick sketch and write the test result in a table. Taking photos of designs at different iterations is also helpful when comparing the results of each version. In design tasks where the test is very fast or it is hard to see every part at once, taking a photo or recording a short video during the test is particularly helpful. An example is seen in Figure 9.3.

During the iterating phase, feedback from people provides valuable information. The designers themselves, peers, the instructor, or anyone else who may be interested, offer insights and suggestions that

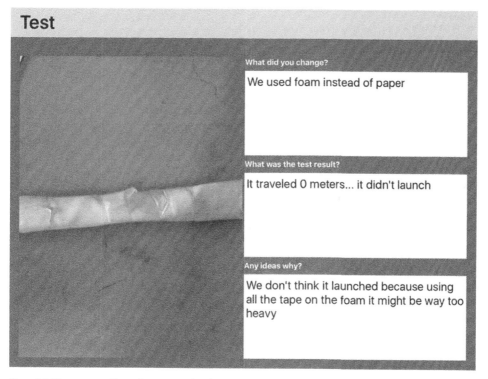

Figure 9.3 Team recording of a test result of a paper stomp rocket.

support the design process. As students iterate, they can complete both self-evaluation forms and peer evaluations. To help students track their evaluations as they iterate, some teachers provide specific prompts for students to record responses on sticky notes (Figure 9.4). Finally, during this phase, students may draw, write, or take pictures to reflect on their process, their teamwork, or their understanding of the process. Examples of types of annotations that can be used to support iteration can be seen in Table 9.2.

Poster Comments

	+ Something I Like	Δ A suggestion for improvement
Description How did the team *describe* their rocket design?	I liked on there first rocket how they made and it looked liked an airplain.	They need to describe more or how they made there goal.
Explanation How did the team *explain* how or why the parts of their rocket make it work?	They had a Lot of reasoning and evidence.	They need to add a littel mor to there last rocket, they need to explain it more

Figure 9.4 Student feedback form for another team's design task poster.

Table 9.2 Types of Annotation to Support the Three Potential Goals in the Iterating Phase

Record Test Results	Get Feedback on Design	Reflect on Process
• Sketch, take photos, or record video of current state of design and test result. • Examine pictures and test results together to draw conclusions from patterns.	• Fill in self- or peer evaluation forms. • Write advice to other teams.	• Fill out teamwork rubric. • Complete written exit ticket of progress made that day.

Sharing Phase

In the sharing phase, students create a representation to share their design, design process, or lessons learned with others not closely involved in their process.

Students may share annotated drawings of the final design, highlighting parts, functions, or materials. Photos offer a clear way to show a design, especially differences between designs that may be difficult to show in drawings. Students may also compose a short narrative about the process, the final design, or another aspect of the activity. For example, this writing or narrative could include instructions for how to use the design, lessons learned that might guide others in the process, or ideas for materials to use in a full-scale version of their design. Examples of types of annotation are in Table 9.3. Figure 9.5 shows a student's reflection on what they learned from another group.

Table 9.3 Types of Annotation That May Support Three Potential Goals in the Sharing Phase

Share Final Design	Share General Design Recommendations	Reflect on and Share Process
• Annotate drawings or photos of final design. • Create instructions for use or building directions for someone to build their own.	• Create whole-class list of design recommendations. • Present poster that shows ways to attach materials.	• Create poster that includes design process noting decisions made from beginning to end. • Present changes that could be included in the next iteration.

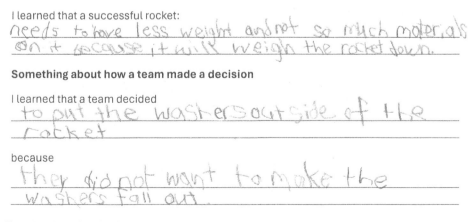

I learned that a successful rocket:

needs to have less weight and not so much materials on it because it will weigh the rocket down.

Something about how a team made a decision

I learned that a team decided

to put the washers outside of the rocket

because

they did not want to make the washers fall out.

Figure 9.5 A student's reflection on what they learned from another team's poster.

Teacher Support

To create their own annotations and documentation, students may need some support from their teacher. We have presented examples here of anchor charts created by the teacher or different forms for students to complete. If the students are familiar with the genre, the teacher simply explains the prompt to get students started. However, if a type of documentation is new, then a full mentor text may be appropriate. Mentor texts are typically full examples of the kind of drawing or writing expected of students. Teachers use mentor texts, for example, when they want to illustrate how to complete a fully annotated drawing on a design. The teacher draws a simple object, such as a chair, shows how to choose the drawing angle, draw arrows to add annotations, and then iterates on the drawing, leading to the final form.

For example, a fourth-grade teacher wanted the students to create a poster at the end of the engineering activity. Because this format was new, the teacher created a mentor text poster displaying the different components of the poster, including the problem statement, final design, a feature of the design, and testing results to show the design process. Before beginning the task, with their teacher's guidance, the students analyzed the different components of the poster. This guidance prepared the students to record the necessary information for their own poster as they worked on the physical design.

This chapter included only a few formats for students to document and share their work. Options for documentation provide students with agency to pick a format suitable to them as well as one that can best tell their design story. In Chapter 11, we discuss different kinds of classroom conversations that can be used in conjunction with writing, drawing, and photographs.

Reference

Museum of Science, Boston. (2015). *Engineering is elementary curriculum units.*

10

Facilitating Engineering Conversations

At the K-8 level, engineering is typically a very hands-on endeavor, with students planning, physically creating, testing, and revising their designs. At the same time, we also want to ensure that students develop engineering knowledge while they are creating their engineering products. Developing this knowledge requires students to interact meaningfully with the ideas of their classmates as they consider more than their own groups' design ideas. Intentionally planned, teacher-facilitated, whole-class conversations are essential to supporting students to think beyond their own designs to other parts of the design process and to engage with other groups' designs. We call these whole-class discussions in engineering "design talks" as a nod to similar structures in math ("number talks") and science talks (Wendell et al., 2024). Design talks are teacher facilitated whole-class or large-group conversations; they are distinctly different from design share-outs, where a single group has the floor at a time and describes their design and/or process. In a design talk, students share their own ideas and listen to others' thinking.

We have found that design talks can invite and leverage different students' strengths in engineering design, which can allow some students to shine. Design talks can be a space to connect students' engineering work to other disciplines, even those outside of STEM, like social studies and language arts. For example, in a social studies unit on ancient civilizations, students could design bridges or irrigation canals using era-appropriate construction methods. Talks around this task could focus on the differences in construction styles between these types of large public-works projects and structures of the same period designed for defense or religious purposes.

DOI: 10.4324/9781003378174-10

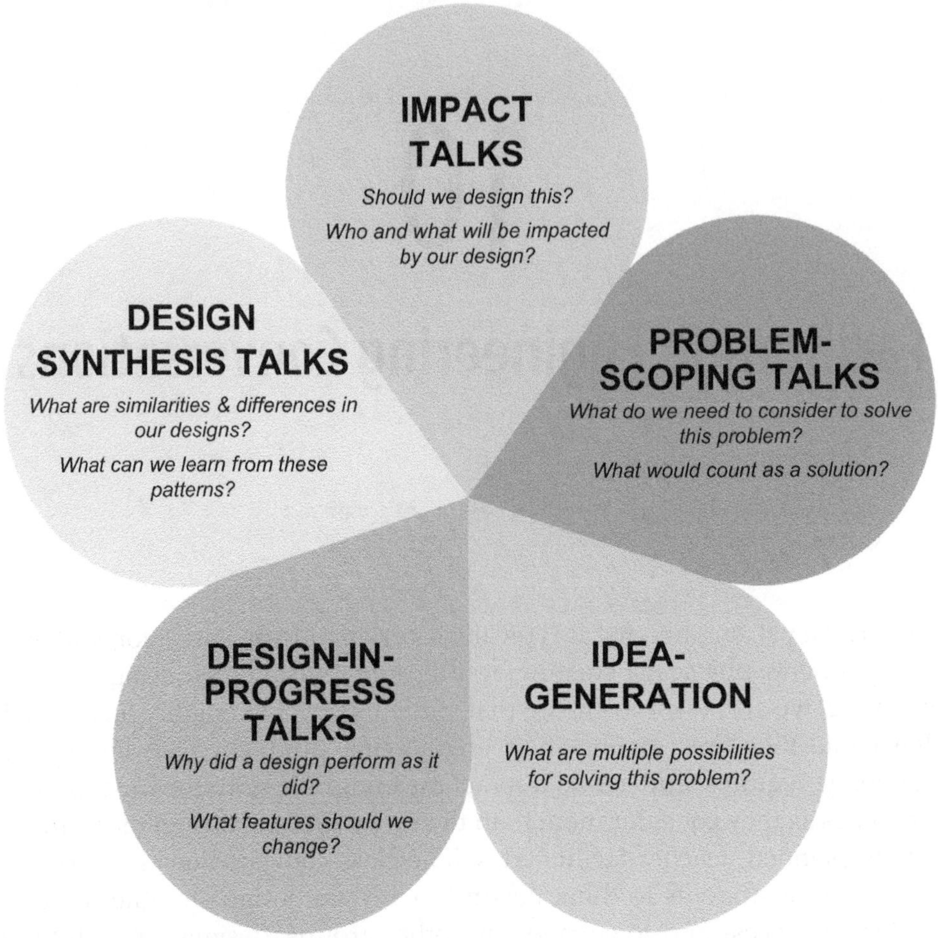

IMPACT TALKS

Should we design this?

Who and what will be impacted by our design?

DESIGN SYNTHESIS TALKS

What are similarities & differences in our designs?

What can we learn from these patterns?

PROBLEM-SCOPING TALKS

What do we need to consider to solve this problem?

What would count as a solution?

DESIGN-IN-PROGRESS TALKS

Why did a design perform as it did?

What features should we change?

IDEA-GENERATION

What are multiple possibilities for solving this problem?

Figure 10.1 Design talk genres.

As in all lesson planning, design talks should connect to instructional goals, including goals for the unit or project, for the day, and for individual students. While design talks can progress in multiple ways, organizing the talks into five genres can enhance the focus and depth of the talks. Figure 10.1 illustrates each genre, problem scoping, idea generation, design-in-progress, design synthesis, and impact, and includes a framing question and specific prompts.

You may notice that some of the genres seem to match up to the stages of a design process and have an intended order. However, the design talk genres are more flexible than they may appear. For example, it may make sense after finishing a design-in-progress talk to have a problem-scoping talk to discuss different ways to think expansively about the problem the students just solved. For example, if students designed bridges, they could respond to the prompt, "If instead of asking you to build a bridge, I had presented a more general problem moving boxes across a river, how would that have changed your process? How could we evaluate the very different designs you might create?" Impact talks can easily stand alone without a construction task involved at all. Design synthesis talks can focus on already-created objects. For example, students could bring in or think of different tools for scrambling eggs and discuss these various existing solutions.

Each of the five design talk genres can be incorporated into many different engineering experiences. For most engineering tasks, one or two design talks is plenty; only the longest engineering unit would attempt to include all five genres. Choose the type of design talk based on your goals. We do not list goals with each genre because many different goals can lead to the same choice of design talk genre. For example, idea generation is useful when students have only a few initial design ideas and equally beneficial when there's an obvious solution and students need to think more broadly.

Design talks do not need to be long to be effective. For kindergarten and first grade, these talks could take less than ten minutes, maybe fifteen by the end of the school year if students have participated in frequent whole-class discussions. For sixth grade, students may discuss a compelling or controversial topic for thirty minutes or more. To enrich discussions, have students share their experiences coupled with artifacts such as impact maps, drawings, lists of criteria and constraints, and even their own or others' physical designs. To help students get started, use common strategies like "turn and talk" or "think-pair-share." If whole-class discussion is not a common routine, some students might need more time to be comfortable with the format, so don't give up if the first attempt feels awkward!

Impact Talks

Impact talks invite students to consider questions like, "Should we design this?", "What are the human and environmental consequences of considering this issue as an engineering design problem?", or "Who might this solution benefit and who might it harm?" As we mentioned, impact talks work well as one-off conversations and do not require students to physically construct anything. This is helpful to show students that engineering thinking does not require building.

Sixth-grade teacher Rae led an impact talk to conclude a social studies unit related to agricultural and hunter-gatherer societies. Students watched a 2019 documentary that focused on a proposed plan to construct a large hydroelectric dam in Brazil, within the Amazon rainforest. Supporting this plan, the Brazilian government claimed the dam would generate affordable electricity and employment, both essential to lifting families out of poverty. However, environmental experts as well as local indigenous people, including the Man-daruku tribe, vehemently opposed construction of the dam because it would flood the forest they live in, forcing them to abandon not only their lifestyle but also the land on which they lived.

Rae crafted an impact talk lesson to help their students problematize the common ideology in our society that technology is always beneficial. They iterated on the lesson several years in a row in response to their students' engagement. In the first year, the prompt was, "Should Brazil build a dam in the Amazon?" As they realized their students needed more structure to under-stand the different perspectives, Rae redesigned the lesson to have students evaluate arguments used by both sides in the documentary. First, students con-sidered the argument given by the Brazilian government (the agricultural soci-ety perspective) to build the dam because life is very difficult for people who do not have electricity. They decided whether this argument was "very strong, strong, weak, or very weak" regardless of their personal view on the dam in general. Next, the students considered the opposite perspective, that of the Mandaruku (the hunter–gatherer perspective). They oppose building the dam; one of their arguments is that it would destroy their culture and livelihood. Again, the students decided if that argument was "very strong, strong, weak, or very weak." Once students had discussed with classmates who shared the same perspective, they came back to the circle for a whole-class discussion.

> Rae: What makes this a strong or weak argument?
>
> Danny: It is a good reason, but they don't have power, so no one's going to listen to them without any more reasons.
>
> Rae: [revoicing this response to ensure other students heard it] The agricultural society has more power than the hunter-gatherer soci-ety. They are going to need more reasons. Why does that matter?
>
> Danny: If they don't have enough power then no one's going to listen to them. They don't have as much power as the agricultural society, so no one's going to listen to them, so they need more reasons for people to listen to them.

Throughout the discussion, students continued to consider the impact of the dam on the various populations as well as the decision-making process regarding building the dam. Students questioned whether the purported ben-efits of the dam would benefit the indigenous populations, since they could not afford the electricity or be hired to build the dam.

Impact talks provide an opportunity for students to understand engi-neering design as a process to help them wrestle with problems from simple to complex and from local to universal. They can realize that engineering design is not always a force for good. Even young children can start to see how engineering often reinforces injustices in local and global contexts (Gunckel & Tolbert, 2018). During impact talks, students reflect on the social, ethical, and moral dimensions of engineering design. With peers, they consider whether design ideas should be implemented, who should have a voice in determining a solution, and what might be unintended consequences of a design.

One way to structure a discussion about the unequal impact of technology is through creating impact maps. To create an impact map, place the technology being considered, which can be an existing or imagined technology, in the center of the diagram. Then, as students think of potential consequences of the technology, both positive and negative, they add them to the map as bubbles connected to the technology. The students then add secondary impacts, to the first level of impacts, and so on. The lines connecting the bubbles can include notes indicating whether the impact is likely to be beneficial or harmful. Another way to structure an impact map is to include who or what is impacted in the bubbles and to write notes about how they are impacted on the connecting lines. Depending on the teacher's goals, the age of the students, and their familiarity with the technology, either students can create impact maps in small groups for a whole-class discussion or the teacher can write one during the discussion, based on what students say. An example impact map written by a middle school teacher during a whole-class discussion is shown in Figure 10.2.

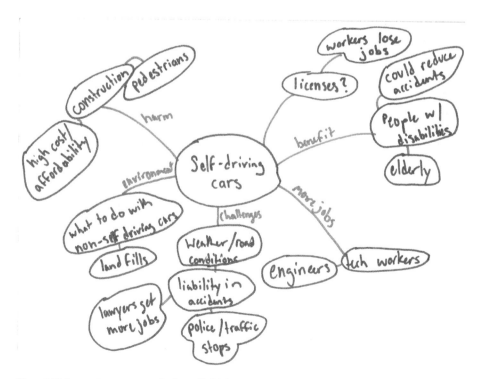

Figure 10.2 Impact map example for self-driving cars.

Problem-Scoping Talks

In problem-scoping talks, students consider questions such as "What do we need to consider when solving this problem?" and "What would count as a solution?" During these talks, students identify and scope design problems with multiple technical, material, and social considerations. While participating in these talks, they think about design constraints and criteria.

Often elementary and middle school teachers grapple with tight schedules, allowing less than optimal time for engineering activities. Therefore, to save time, teachers may present a list of criteria and constraints to students rather than having students do the problem scoping themselves. As a result, when beginning a problem-scoping talk, students may need assurance that their ideas will be considered and that the purpose of the talk is not to simply guess the list that the teacher has generated; rather, the teacher should encourage as much creative brainstorming around the problem as possible.

In one problem-scoping talk, Naina, a fifth-grade science teacher, wanted students to think through a design task to keep pollutants out of a storm drain on the side of a road. Students quickly agreed they needed to block the pollution, but they also realized the water still needed to flow into the drain to prevent flooding. Naina then prompted them to consider success criteria. Does all the pollution need to be removed? The students thought that, yes, ideally, all the pollution should be trapped, but realistically, they expected some of it would get through. They debated whether it would be better if a design trapped all the pollution and blocked some of the water or if a design allowed all of the water to go through but also allowed some of the pollution into the drain.

Naina showed students a picture of rainbow-hued oil flowing into a storm drain. She asked the students if they wanted to test their designs with the actual oil pollutants. Students rejected using real motor oil and then wondered aloud what the most authentic but safe substitute would be. Once they agreed to use cooking oil, one student suggested adding soap to the design to remove the oil it encountered since soap is used to remove grease from a pan. The class then debated the merits of adding soap. Would soap be considered an additional pollutant once it hit the waterway? If so, is the soap a less harmful pollutant than the oil?

This conversation offered opportunities for students to consider many aspects of the problem, including how to model oil in a classroom, how to determine success criteria for a design, and how to define pollution in a waterway. In the end, thinking through the criteria and constraints of the design task amplified students' understanding and ownership of the task. In the problem-scoping talk involving the turtle egg transport device in Chapter 6, Vera's students also considered ethical and political contexts of sea turtle egg protection.

Problem-scoping talks help students think about solutions to problems, reflecting on the perspectives and needs of the people and environment who will be affected. This genre of design talk includes conversations about physical criteria and constraints, and often leads to rich conversations about values, ethics, and design priorities.

Idea-Generation Talks

In idea-generation talks, the whole class collectively generates multiple design ideas, using prompts such as "What are multiple possibilities for solving the problem?" or "How have people and animals solved similar problems?" Depending on the teacher's goals, the students' familiarity with engineering, and the task, these large-group talks can precede, follow, or replace individual or small-group idea-generation activities. By brainstorming in a large group, students share ideas to solve a problem, listen to and build off other's contributions, and weigh the pros and cons of different perspectives.

A first-grade teacher, Molly, posed the problem of kindergarteners having difficulty using the monkey bar structure on the school playground. To address the Next Generation Science Standards related to mimicking plant and animal parts, Molly suggested that the students try a biomimetic design approach to come up with solutions. She displayed a collage of photos of animals and plants that excel at climbing, reaching, sticking, and jumping such as a gecko, a sloth, a frog, or a climbing vine plant. Students brainstormed in response to the following prompt: "These pictures of plants and animals give you some ideas of what we could design for the kindergarteners to help them play on that play structure. What do you notice?"

During the idea-generation talk, the students shared a range of ideas. First, three students suggested providing the children with 1) gloves with sticky features like a gecko's toes, 2) attachments for shoes that would enable jumping like a frog, or 3) stretchy gloves that would let you glide like a flying squirrel. Another student connected these ideas by noting that if the jumping shoes gave the kindergarteners too much motion, the sticky gloves could help them stick to the monkey bars once they got there. Other students cautioned against overly sticky gloves that would impede swinging across the bars. They suggested adding a switch with a battery that could block some of the sticky sections when you wanted to swing to a new bar (Figure 10.3).

As the conversation continued, students brainstormed more design solutions, clarifying, refining, and combining ideas. Following this idea-generation talk, students sketched their design ideas. In this activity, Molly chose sketching instead of building because she wanted her first-grade students to be able to think of and visualize many complex ideas and not be limited to what they could build. With teacher facilitation, idea-generation talks can create an environment in which one student's idea can spark other students, enabling students to build ideas collectively. This structure supports the norm that ideas in the classroom are not private property but rather are meant to be shared so that everyone can learn from all the ideas.

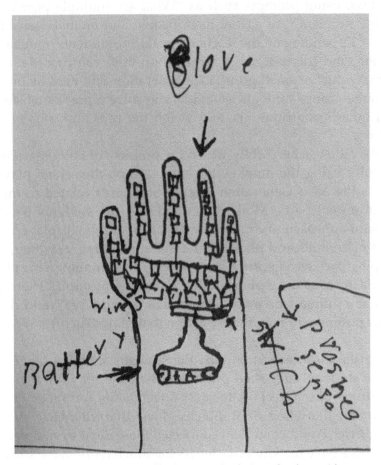

Figure 10.3 Student drawing of brainstormed solution of a glove with a battery and pressure sensor switch.

Design-in-Progress Talks

In design-in-progress talks, students reflect on, "Why did a design perform as it did?" and "What features should we change?" Since these talks typically interrupt students' physical construction and testing, the talks must directly benefit the design work; the focus of design-in-progress talks should be on helping students solve design problems.

In a fourth-grade classroom working on paper stomp rockets, the teacher noticed that many students were having similar struggles with their designs. During testing of the rocket designs, the top of the rocket, made of small paper cups, often flew off or separated from the cylindrical body of the rocket. Hence, the teacher ended the building session with a design-in-progress talk to get students to pause, look at each other's rockets, and think of solutions together. To begin the talk, the students shared their design problems. The teacher recorded short versions of their responses on a white board (Figure 10.4). Then, the students contributed ideas on what to change about the designs to address these common problems. Students spent ten minutes sharing ideas about ways to improve the designs.

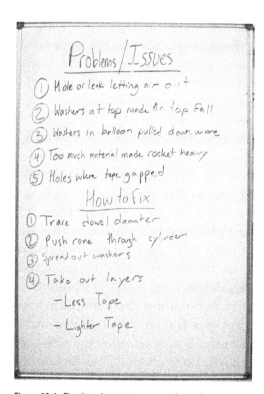

Figure 10.4 Design-in-progress anchor chart.

Design-in-progress talks allow students to slow down their building and consider the pros and cons of specific design features. Students move beyond the "show-and-tell" of their own designs and even go beyond sharing views on their peers' designs. These conversations encourage students to think like engineers as they reflect together on the mechanisms of all the groups' designs.

Design Synthesis Talks

Design synthesis talks support students to reason across their designs and synthesize common themes, using prompts such as "What are similarities and differences in our designs?" and "What can we learn from these patterns?". These talks typically occur after students create and test a range of design solutions. A synthesis talk can occur without students creating their own designs first. This involves examining, comparing, and contrasting real-world designs intended to solve the same problem. Unlike share-out sessions, which resemble design show and tell, design synthesis talks enhance practice in synthesizing information and analytic reasoning.

The purpose of design synthesis talks varies, often depending on how similar the different designs are. Sometimes students discuss how designs differ in how they serve the same function but use different structures. Other times, students reflect on the differences in the general interpretation of the problem or in the specific criteria and constraints.

A boat design task offered an opportunity for students to discuss trade-offs during a design synthesis talk. For example, in one after-school workshop, we challenged students to transport an egg across a tub of water with a fan blowing across the surface to model wind. (Note that we intentionally did not use the word "boat" as that might have limited ideas; students were inspired by everything from inflatable pool floats, inner tubes, rafts, and sailboats to container ships.) Transporting an egg "passenger" was a broad task. As students began exploring within this open design space, they began to create their own mini challenges within the task. Different students were curious about the number of eggs a transporter could carry at one time, the maximum speed of the egg transporter, or ways to propel a transporter without the fan. After all teams had been successful moving at least one egg across the bin, we realized that the wide range of solutions created a perfect opportunity for a design synthesis talk.

We asked each team to summarize their results on an index card, including the number of eggs transported, the speed of the transporter, and any other important information. The students placed their designs and the index cards in the middle of the circle of students. The facilitator gave students an open-ended prompt: "These are all such cool designs. And they are all so different! I wonder if we can compare the different designs and the results to make conclusions about egg transporter designs." Some students quickly pointed out that lighter designs went faster; one student argued that the lighter transporters were also all smaller, so it was hard to know whether weight or size mattered more.

The group that challenged themselves to carry as many eggs as possible stated that their wide, flat design held the most eggs because it was the most stable. Another group pointed out that while that design held many eggs, it was also the slowest. The students briefly debated whether it was slow because it was wide and flat or because it was carrying so much more weight than the other transporters. One group inspired by a kayak had made the narrowest transporter. Since their design was the opposite of the wide, flat design, they suggested comparing the two. The kayak group pointed out that while their design was fast, as they had hoped, it was not very useful because it was unstable; it constantly tipped over before traveling the length of the bin. The students wondered if they could create the "best" transporter, which they seemed to define as in between these two extremes, stable and able to carry a load but also fast. To help them think more expansively, the facilitator pointed out that maybe there was no single best transporter design; in the real world, we have many water transporter designs, each optimized for different purposes.

In this conversation, students compared all the designs to make general claims about a water transporter design. The many different designs allowed them to synthesize multiple perspectives, organize diverse information, and filter the most meaningful data. Because they had different priorities for their designs, they could compare the designs without feeling competitive. Even though the groups mostly focused on their own designs, the facilitators noted that the groups listened and responded to the ideas of the other groups. They built off their ideas, pushed back on conclusions, and even offered additional nuance to claims.

In this chapter, we discussed five kinds of teacher-facilitated whole-class design talks in which students deepen their reasoning about design problems, prototypes, and impacts. We provided possible prompts that target the specific purpose of each genre of design talk: problem-scoping, idea-generation, design-in-progress, design synthesis, and impact. In some cases, students focus the discussion on a tangible artifact, while other times they grapple with conceptual ideas. The teacher has a specific role in these talks, to encourage students to reason and revoice ideas and help students connect their insights with others'.

References

Gunckel, K. L., & Tolbert, S. (2018). The imperative to move toward a dimension of care in engineering education. *Journal of Research in Science Teaching*, 55(7), 938–961.

Wendell, K., Watkins, J., Andrews, C., Pangan, T., DeLucca, N., Gor, V., Malinowski, M., Sood, N., & Woodcock, R. (2024). Design talks: Whole-class conversations during engineering design units. *Science & Children*, 61(1), 64–69. https://doi.org/10.1080/00368148.2023.2292391.

11

Inclusive and Connected Engineering Classrooms

Throughout this book, we have presented case studies, strategies, research, and examples of engineering practices that support student learning and growth. For example, through engineering, students can develop problem-solving, reasoning, and creative thinking skills. Engineering can also help build inclusive classroom communities that value the varied backgrounds and skills of all students. Additionally, while learning engineering, students can develop skills related to executive functioning and social-emotional learning. For example, while testing a design, students must manage their frustration when a device does not work and then collaborate with their peers as they decide next steps. While the first two parts of this book focus on understanding and creating engineering opportunities in K-8 classrooms, this chapter looks at engineering in ways that meet the needs of all students. The chapter includes specific strategies and suggestions for teachers to create inclusive engineering classrooms.

Access to engineering and its resources is often not equitable from school to school or even within a school. Some students may not ever get the chance to explore engineering; other students may have an opportunity to do engineering, but they must work within rigid guidelines with few choices. More affluent schools often offer engineering opportunities and can afford more expensive materials. In schools that are not as privileged, many see engineering as something only for gifted or "high ability" learners, which often excludes other students (Cohen, 2022). It is no surprise that a higher percentage of students identified as gifted are white. Additionally, some students are not included in engineering sessions because they have goals that take them

DOI: 10.4324/9781003378174-11

out of the class, such as some multilingual students or those who receive special education services. Not only do gifted students generally receive more engineering time than other students, but education researchers also often spend the most time studying students in gifted classrooms.

Meeting Students Where They Are

With an emphasis on problem solving, creativity, and discovery, engineering offers all students an opportunity to enjoy and thrive as they participate in engineering activities. The openness of engineering design is well-suited to meeting the needs of students with different abilities, experiences, and backgrounds. Many scaffolds for students can be designed during the activity planning process.

Universal Design for Learning (UDL) offers a useful framework for situating equity in the engineering classroom. The goal of UDL is "to improve and optimize teaching and learning for all people based on scientific insights into how humans learn" (CAST, 2018). UDL guidelines say that there is no one way that people learn best and that even the same person may approach learning differently depending on the day or the activity; therefore, what is good for one may not be good for all. UDL principles include concrete suggestions for designing learning with multiple options to support equitable access and participation. For example, a checklist can aid those students who need executive functioning and organization support during the EDP. UDL outlines three strands for supporting students to 1) **engage** or motivate, 2) **represent** their ideas or comprehend information, and 3) **express** their ideas.

As a note, UDL is different from providing individual students with accommodations through an Individualized Education Plan (IEP). With UDL, learning approaches are available to all students in a class, not just to the students who have been identified as needing specific support. To be clear, we are not saying that during engineering time, students' IEPs should be disregarded. As with IEP accommodations, proactively making resources available to students helps them take ownership of their learning as they decide which strategies are most useful to them at different times.

How to Help Students Access the Engineering Curriculum

Like all classroom activities, planning and facilitating engineering requires teachers to consider various aspects. Responsive teaching and design talks can provide in-the-moment support for students to not only think deeply and creatively but also express their ideas with confidence and clarity. Anticipating what might happen in the classroom allows teachers to respond quickly in the moment as they have played out various scenarios to help students move toward greater independence and engagement. Planning the scaffolds students may need and deciding when to offer them can equip students with the necessary tools to manage their work more independently and confidently.

In short, to figure out what options are right for your class, anticipate how the class and individual students may react to an activity. One way to figure out what types of conversations and resources might benefit students is to complete a journey map to show how learners may proceed through an activity. This is a UDL planning strategy for educators. When planning an activity, map out the steps of the activity in detail. It's useful to use sticky notes and physically map it out. Next, identify pain points and curriculum barriers that might keep students from being able to access the activity. Once the steps and barriers are clear, think about the resources and conversations for supporting the students. This is a very short synopsis of journey mapping, a planning activity tool that many educators find valuable.

How to Enhance Student Engagement in the Engineering Design Process

◆ Classroom norms: Review established classroom norms or establish new engineering norms. (See Chapter 4 for a review of norms specific to engineering.)

◆ Discussions and feedback sessions: Use whole-class and small-group discussions to hear about students' past experiences, make sure all students understand necessary concepts, and support students to build new skills.

  – Discussing the engineering concepts prior to starting the activity helps all students begin with a common foundation.

  – Modeling new practices supports students' skills in giving and receiving peer feedback. For example, if students are asked to iterate their designs based on feedback, model what this looks like using a similar scenario during a design-in-progress design talk.

  – Practicing "turn and talk" prior to whole-class discussions. This promotes students' confidence to participate in whole-class discussions. With turn and talk, students talk to a partner one-on-one before they share with the whole class. This approach gives all students time to organize their ideas, but it is particularly beneficial for English language learners or students who need increased processing time.

◆ Language access: Talk about key terms, vocabulary, and concepts to make sure all students share a common language for discussion. Review words such as *iteration, constraints*, and *criteria* or any essential technical terms.

   – Be mindful of students' identities and how they may use certain words or phrases. They may use words in ways that don't align with the word's formal definition to express their thoughts. This is okay. Try to understand the idea they are trying to convey and respond to the idea. This is more important than making sure they are using terminology correctly. Correcting students when they are trying to express themselves may make them hesitant to share their ideas later.

◆ Collaboration guidelines: Students need guidance on how best to participate with other students or in groups. Take time to discuss norms for group and pair work and provide time to practice this teamwork. For example, talk about a problem and then show students two different solutions; then, guide students to ask questions, give feedback, and negotiate which design idea to pursue. Use the collaboration norms to discuss what went well with the process and what could be improved.

◆ Frustration: Acknowledge that building and working with others can be frustrating at times. Offer students strategies to manage frustration if it comes up. Options include walking away for a few minutes, asking a partner to clarify their ideas, or recruiting the teacher or another student for help.

◆ Materials: Offer a variety of materials to make sure all students have experience using some of them. Give students time to explore the materials prior to planning. Understanding the properties of the materials boosts confidence and enhances collaboration.

◆ Checklists: Use checklists to support students as they move through stages of the engineering design process. Checklists may focus on steps of the EDP and incorporating constraints and criteria into the design.

◆ Engineering skills: Start with more structured activities in terms of engineering, social, and organizational aspects and move to more open-ended ones. Building foundational skills ensures that students understand open-ended activities, provides a uniform starting point, and supports student agency.

◆ Processing time: Build in time for students to process their ideas and those of others. Have students jot down their ideas first or provide worksheets to guide them.

Problem Context

Differences in students' experiences and skills can lead to imbalances in knowledge, either real or perceived. Teachers can implement strategies to ensure that all students begin activities feeling equally prepared. Picking a familiar context is one way to minimize these imbalances. Settings such as schools, neighborhoods, or other places and situations common to the students work well. However, when activity contexts are unfamiliar, there are ways to build the necessary contextual knowledge. One way is to ask more directed questions to assess the students' understandings of a concept or context. Students' answers can guide teachers in deciding what additional information to provide so that everyone understands the topic or context.

Problem Selection

Sometimes teachers select the problem for students, and other times, students select the problem. Although students are excited when they get to choose, providing guidelines is helpful because some students struggle with seemingly unlimited choices. One guideline is to provide a context for the problem such as home or school. It is also okay to share a few problems that can be used as jumping-off ideas.

Students may identify several problems but after discussion realize that some problems cannot be solved in the classroom. For example, a water transportation system for the desert makes sense, but students could not fully execute this solution in the classroom. Therefore, once the class generates a list of problems, teachers can lead a whole-class discussion or work with groups to categorize problems into two groups: 1) problems that engineering can solve given the available time and materials of the classroom and 2) problems that require time or materials that are not available. This process may require teacher guidance and prompting questions since students may not have the experience to realistically gauge the classroom constraints of time and materials.

Problem Scoping

When students begin problem scoping, consider two questions: 1) Is this a problem that all students will understand? 2) Will they have experiences that they can draw on? If the context or problem is new, students may have difficulty organizing all the information needed when beginning to plan a solution. We suggest providing multiple ways to help them organize their thinking as they scope the problem, such as the following:

◆ Present problems in a variety of ways with robust descriptions of the problem and clients. Providing a design brief can support classroom discussion and remind students of information once they start working.

◆ Offer short readings and/or videos to create an understanding of the problem.

◆ Give students time to ask questions about the problem scenario and have students brainstorm answers together.

◆ Provide an outline of a design brief or a planning document and fill in information during the activity introduction and discussion. This can include information such as client, client's needs, constraints, and criteria. Student planning documents are available in Appendix A.

Planning

The first step in planning is to ensure that students are familiar and comfortable with the available materials and have an opportunity to manipulate them.

◆ Create a checklist of the materials so students can better organize their work. Also offer planning worksheets with a checklist to help students keep track of their work; some students benefit from receiving the planning document in one or two sections at a time.

◆ Allow students to share their design ideas in a variety of ways. Options include planning sheets, demonstrations of how something will work, videos, and labeled drawings or sketches.

◆ Ask students to explain their design choices and how their solution will work. Sometimes the simple prompt of "How will it work?" triggers the students to think about the mechanisms they need to build.

◆ Give students sticky notes to jot down design or solution ideas as they brainstorm. For some students, recording on sticky notes is less formal and hence less intimidating than completing a planning document.

◆ Share examples of what already exists in the "real" world to initiate brainstorming. Have the class or groups share ideas in a round robin.

◆ Provide a dry erase board divided into sections with a solution idea in each section. To narrow down choices, groups work together to list positive and negative aspects of each.

◆ Remind students of norms for working together. For example, the goal of the planning process is to select the most feasible solution together; therefore, collaboration is preferred over competition.

Building

Students' experiences with building will vary by the amount of time they have spent doing hands-on building and by the materials they have used. Some students may have no prior experience with building.

◆ Involve students in short skill-building activities to learn about the properties of the materials and how they may connect to each other.

◆ Have students name properties of the materials when they are introduced.

◆ Provide some premade components such as gears, pulleys, wheels, and axles.

◆ Act as an extra set of hands, following the students' directions.

Testing Physical Solutions

Testing is a bit tricky when students are building solutions to different problems or their solutions to the same problem are highly diverse. Here are some suggestions to address this challenge.

◆ If students are building similar solutions, set up a testing station and model how they should test. For example, a central testing station works well when students are making a stomp rocket fly. There are often multiple solutions to this challenge, but the testing is similar.

◆ Offer testing sheets so students can track data. These sheets might need to be customized based on designs if students are building different solutions or are working on different problems. An example testing sheet is included in Appendix B.

◆ Remind students that they may become frustrated when solutions do not work as anticipated and offer some tips to manage the frustration such as taking a quick break. Remind them that testing is a way to get information about their design and that failure is a necessary part of the design process.

◆ If a design does not work at all or does not work the way students envisioned, they often want to take the entire thing apart. If the solution is not working, demonstrate how to analyze the design and problem by looking at the little parts rather than taking the whole solution apart.

Feedback Sessions

Different teachers incorporate different strategies for students to give each other feedback. We encourage teachers to create norms around feedback sessions. Ron Berger's guidelines for feedback asks student to provide feedback that is "kind, specific, and useful" (Berger et al., 2016; Expeditionary Learning, 2024). We'll talk about four that we've seen work well in classrooms:

- ◆ Glow and grow: When giving feedback, students share one thing that they appreciate about another group's design (glow) and one idea for improvement (grow).
- ◆ Gallery walk—version 1: Students walk around the room looking at each other's designs, leaving written feedback for each group on paper or sticky notes.
- ◆ Gallery walk—version 2: One person from each group stays with the group's creation and talks with class members as they rotate through each group's design. Then, there is another round as the people staying with the designs visit each group's design.
- ◆ Presentation: Presentations work well when students have a clear understanding of the format of the presentation. Groups can be given a choice of what type of visual(s) they would like to present in addition to speaking.

Iterating

Students may need support to think about what parts of their design can be improved and how to make changes. Often students think they are done after their first version of a design or want to take apart their entire device if one part doesn't work.

- ◆ Remind students to pick one thing about their design to work on at a time as they iterate. Help them interpret their testing data to figure out what to change.
- ◆ Dry erase boards and sticky notes can be used as tools during group conversations for students to decide what is working about the design and what needs to be changed.
- ◆ Teacher-provided prompts such as "What parts are working well?" and "What is one thing that you would like to change?" can guide conversations when students begin iterating.

Communicating Information

Considering the students' goals and comfort levels, try various sharing formats throughout the design process.

◆ Allow students to choose a preferred format to share their initial planning ideas or a final product. Choose formats that showcase the same information but build student agency. Examples include presentations, print or web advertisements, short videos, or written directions on how to implement the solution.

◆ If students are more comfortable communicating nonverbally, use formats like short videos or rough cartoon sequences for them to demonstrate their ideas.

◆ Use different ways for students to share feedback aside from whole-class presentations. For example, one group of students shares with another group and gets feedback for a specified amount of time and then they switch roles. Another option is to combine small-group conversations with gallery walks. In this case, one person from a design team stays with their design as the other members walk around to see other groups' designs. The person who stays with the design shares their design ideas and answers questions. Ensure that there is time to switch roles. The students who walk around ask questions and give feedback, either verbally or on sticky notes that stay with the design.

In-the-Moment Support

Although the goal is to plan and provide students with scaffolds, observing students with an activity provides ongoing, valuable information. When students are having difficulties, step back and assess the root of the issue. Figure out where the disconnect is and provide students with tools so they can manage independently and move forward.

When delivering support in the moment, consider four aspects: activity framing and context, engineering content, social-emotional learning, and executive functioning. First determine which aspect is most challenging; then determine what scaffolds to introduce. According to UDL values, scaffolds that help one student will most likely benefit others. Reflecting on the question posed in Figure 11.1 can help identify students' needs and associated support. After understanding these needs, work with students to choose the appropriate support as a resource.

Activity Framing and Context

◆ Do students understand the context of the activity and your directions?

◆ Do you need to provide more or different information?

ASSESSING WHAT STUDENTS NEED & WHAT KIND OF SUPPORT TO OFFER

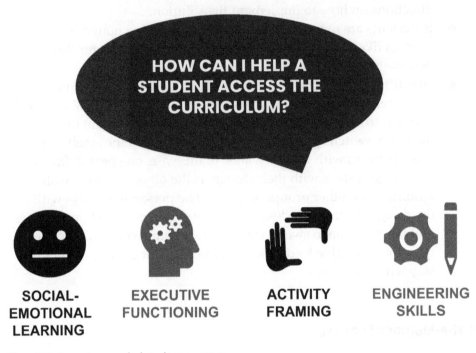

Figure 11.1 Assessing needed student support.

Engineering Content

◆ Do students understand the engineering-specific information necessary for the task?
◆ Do students understand how to use the materials?

Social-Emotional Learning

◆ Are students productively interacting with each other?
◆ Do students seem stuck and/or frustrated?

Executive Functioning

◆ Have students come up with ideas but are not moving forward?

Admittedly, introducing open-ended engineering is not as easy as doing highly constrained and structured activities. The benefit is that students have agency, feel valued, learn how to manage frustration, and experience more genuine interactions with the engineering design process. With planning, teachers have more time to connect and talk more with students while they are working independently with their peers. By approaching engineering from a UDL standpoint and anticipating students' needs and issues, teachers have strategies and scaffolds ready for quick implementation to leverage students' strengths. After a few engineering experiences, both teachers and students find the process easier, with students showing greater agency as they select scaffolds and strategies that best suit them.

References

Berger, R., Woodfin, L, & Vilen, A. (2016). *Learning that lasts: Challenging, engaging, and empowering students with deeper instruction.* San Francisco, CA: Jossey-Bass.

CAST. (2018). *Universal design for learning guidelines version 2.2.* http://udlguidelines.cast.org.

Cohen, K. (2022). Young, gifted, and black: Inequitable outcomes of gifted and talented programs. *Journal of Public and International Affairs.* https://jpia.princeton.edu/news/young-gifted-and-black-inequitable-outcomes-gifted-and-talented-programs.

Expeditionary Learning. (2024). *Critique and Feedback.* https://eleducation.org/resources/critique-and-feedback.

12

Choosing Materials and Building

In this chapter, we are going to discuss considerations of material selection. We will address choosing and presenting materials as well as introduce strategies to balance students' differing experiences with materials. We'll also discuss how to use planning documents to scaffold the way students think about materials.

Anticipating Problems

As you select materials, anticipate the problems students might identify as well as solutions they could build with the materials. For example, if students are building something to help the main character in *A Long Walk to Water* by Linda Sue Parks, carry water to and from a pond, you will need to offer waterproof materials. For another activity about Abby, a dog that has lost the use of her hind legs, consider solutions that help Abby move from one place to another; in this case, students might need wheels to build a cart or a prosthetic for Abby. Planning for potential solutions and the necessary accompanying materials can help students to design solutions that realize their ideas.

Choosing Materials

There is not one perfect set of materials to use; beyond anticipating solutions, there are other factors to consider, such as cost, ease and speed of learning, functionality, and student experience. If materials are familiar,

DOI: 10.4324/9781003378174-12

versatile, and easy to use, students can more readily envision how to use them in a design. Common in makerspaces, high-tech tools such as 3D printers and laser cutters are not necessary for students to create solutions. They tend to be expensive and take longer for students to learn how to use. Although these tools allow students to build more realistic and functional projects, they are not essential unless they meet certain goals. For instance, some teachers would like their students to become adept with these tools, and they carve out extra time for this instruction. Next, we'll talk about craft/recyclables, robotics, and commercially available engineering kits.

Craft, Office, and Recyclable Materials

We've seen endless possibilities for craft, office, and recyclable materials in classrooms. Customize this list according to the needs and experience of the students once they start to do various engineering activities.

Craft and Office Supplies
- tape
- glue
- aluminum foil
- wire
- modeling clay
- pipe cleaners
- dowel rods
- rubber bands
- string
- pennies or something that can act as a weight
- Velcro
- glue gun (with teacher assistance if necessary)
- cardboard scissors (with teacher assistance if necessary)

Recyclable
- cardboard boxes—variety of boxes of different weights and sizes
- chipboard & cereal boxes
- recycled plastic containers
- cloth
- paper towel tubes

The benefits of using recyclable materials are that they are inexpensive and easy to restock. Some teachers send a letter home to families asking for donations. In general, we do not suggest asking families for donations since all families may not be able to participate, but in this case, everyone has recyclable materials so that all students can contribute. (See Sample Letter to Families in Appendix F.) Since students are familiar with these materials, which are abundant and readily available, they are more likely to create multiple iterations.

Constraints include the limitations presented by the restricted functionality of some of these materials. Therefore, students might lean toward building representational designs rather than functional ones. Teachers need to emphasize that they are looking for functional designs, ones that work. In the following example, two sixth-grade students discuss creating a cart to transport water for a character in *A Long Walk to Water* as part of a Novel Engineering unit. The teacher asked the class to build functional designs and then demonstrate how they would work. Luis and Amani have drawn a cart and begin to discuss the materials they will use.

Luis:	Okay, I was thinking we would use soda bottle lids for the wheels and glue them on the side of the cart.
Amani:	But they wouldn't roll, and that seems like the wheels would be really small. How big did you think the cart would be?
Luis:	Umm. I was thinking it would be about this big [uses a finger and his thumb to show about four inches].
Amani:	That seems really small. We wouldn't really be able to test it out to see if it can carry water.
Luis:	What are you thinking?
Amani:	How about this big? [uses her hands to show a span of about three feet]
Luis:	That is much bigger. I'm not sure what we would use for wheels.
Amani:	I thought we could use one of the cardboard boxes and put wheels on that. Maybe we could use cardboard for the wheels too.
Luis:	I bet we could make wheels, but . . . how would we attach them?
Amani:	We could put a hole in the middle of them and use one of the dowel rods like an axle. Right? But then we have to attach that.
Luis:	We can't tape the axle because it couldn't spin. What about taping the paper towel tube or something like that?
Amani:	So tape the tube on the box and then put the dowel inside of that?

Luis goes over to the materials table and brings back a box, a dowel rod, and a paper towel tube. He put the materials together without taping them to show Amaini what he means.

Luis: Yes, that's what I was thinking.

Amani: I like that. And it will really work.

In this next example, Luis and Amani refined their design idea as they discussed which materials they wanted to use. They built the cart and put it on the floor to test it. The wheels were a little wobbly, but the cart rolled.

Luis: It works! Should we put some weight in it so we can see if it will hold something heavy?

Amani: Yes, definitely.

Amani gets a few textbooks and puts them in the cart. Luis pulls it. A couple of the wheels splay out, so the cart is not able to roll.

Amani: Uh-oh. That doesn't work.

Luis: It sort of worked. I think it was too much weight. We need to change something.

Amani: They did work with no weight.

They start to manipulate the cardboard discs they have to cut to be the wheels.

Luis: What if they are thicker, the wheels?

Amani: That might work. Should we see if we can have more cardboard?

They cut eight more circles and glued two more to each of the existing wheels to make the wheels thicker. They tested and decided to add two more circles to each wheel. This time, the cart held weight without the wheels splaying out. Since they were using recycled materials, there was enough cardboard for them to have more. It was also very easy for them to change the wheel design by using a glue gun and extra cardboard. In this case, wheels made on a 3D printer or laser cutter would have been sturdier but would have required additional time because the students had never used those tools. With craft materials, the students were able to quickly make changes.

Given their budget and available time, many teachers prefer to mix craft, office, and recyclable materials. These materials allow the students to jump right into building without spending time learning to use more complicated technologies. When using these materials, it is helpful to remind students that they are completing functional designs that should incorporate the constraints and criteria already outlined.

Robotics

There are various robotics platforms that can be used in K-8 classrooms. Some of the platforms have a programming component, while others do not require any programming. These kits often include a programmable brick, sensors, motors, and interlocking building bricks. Regardless of the platform, schedule time for students to become familiar with the tools and programming in the kits.

The benefits of these kits include that the materials are reusable. Additionally, building with robotics allows students to easily iterate on designs and create sturdy structures. Including motors and/or sensors allows students to build functional designs easily. For example, if students want to build an alarm system, they could use a light sensor that activates a motor attached to a bell.

Constraints of robotics include both cost and time. Although kits are available at various price points, staffing a classroom can be expensive. Furthermore, costly robotics kits may be accessible to some students but not others. The variability in experience with these materials can lead to inequities. For example, those students who've had access may mold designs to fit the materials they've previously used. In one fourth-grade classroom, a pair of boys wanted to make a robotic car. Familiar with robotics, they specifically chose a problem anticipating a solution requiring a robotic car. Finally, time is a constraint since learning these new tools can be time consuming.

Packaged Engineering Kits

There are several engineering kits that come as part of curricula. These kits include materials used for all activities in the curriculum or sets of specific ones that are used for individual activities. While we will not address specific engineering curricula, we will discuss some of the benefits and constraints of premade kits.

The benefits of using commercially available kits include saving time by offering materials that were already collected and organized. In addition, the kits usually come with a menu of activities that work well with the materials. If activities need materials with specific properties, they are included in the premade kits. For example, if there is a problem that includes water, materials will include waterproof items.

The constraints of these kits tend to outweigh their benefits. Materials for each activity are specific and could hamper students' creativity and lead to a lack of diversity between groups' designs. In addition, with a specific set of materials on hand, students may tailor their designs to these materials instead of using their own ideas for inspiration. Additionally, similar to robotics, these kits are expensive to restock and maintain.

Material Considerations and Planning for Use

When planning a unit, think about when to introduce the materials, when to allow students to gather them, and how much previous experience students have had with the materials. Furthermore, think about how to provide the most equitable experience for students and best support their planning processes.

Introducing Materials

Available materials can be introduced before, during, or after planning. Introducing materials at different points in the design process presents both benefits and drawbacks. Table 12.1 details the advantages and disadvantages of presenting materials at different times in the process. However, let students

Table 12.1 When to Introduce Materials

	Potential Benefits	Potential Drawbacks
BEFORE PLANNING	Greater chance of innovation of ideas. Lower chance of students feeling unable to plan since they don't know which materials they will be using.	Students may need to change their plan if available materials won't work. Students may pick design based on materials. Students may design based on perceived material properties.
DURING PLANNING	Greater chance of innovation. Students do not base their design around available materials.	Students may not understand the potential of materials, which may limit design ideas.
AFTER PLANNING	Students may find innovative ways to work with materials so they fit with the planned design.	Students may need to change their designs to fit with available materials.

know early on which materials are available so they can plan designs that align to what they can actually build. Also, creating the space for students to explore materials fosters equity, confidence, and deeper engagement. Make sure that students have a list of materials and see, touch, and explore them so they know what they will work with.

A materials catalog is a creative and efficient way to present materials. A basic materials catalog has the name and a picture of each item. A catalog can also include different uses for materials, pictures of materials that have been used as part of a design, and methods of connecting different materials. Some teachers compile and present the catalog to the class to spark creativity. Others have their students generate the catalog to serve as a way for students to collaborate and share knowledge.

Gathering Materials

Student groups will not all plan at the same pace. Therefore, during the planning process, let them know at what point they will be able to get materials. Telling students that they can get materials after they have finished their plan may give an advantage to groups who plan more quickly. In these cases, the groups who finish first have access to all materials while groups who spend more time planning have a more limited selection. These groups may even have to alter their designs to adjust to the remaining materials. There are several strategies to support those students who need more planning time. When students need more planning time, teachers can remind the ones who finished planning earlier not to:

- ◆ hoard materials as they work.
- ◆ take materials before their teacher has approved the designs and materials list.
- ◆ take materials for more than one specific section when there are multiple components in their designs.
- ◆ keep materials they are not using at their seats instead of returning them as quickly as possible.

Guiding Students in Selecting and Using Materials

Students with more experience with materials can better anticipate how certain materials will function in their designs. If the materials are new to students, have them first experiment with them. Either add time to the planned activity or do a preliminary stand-alone activity. Chapter 8 contains several introductory activities for students to become familiar with materials.

Since students differ in the ways they use and plan with materials, keep planning structures flexible. For example, some students prefer to manipulate materials while brainstorming. Others may want to conduct mini tests to see how specific materials perform or how different materials can be connected. Some students may simply discuss the materials with their partner with or without a planning document. In all cases, the priority is to ensure students are engaged creatively in sharing their ideas.

Planning documents help students scaffold their thinking about what materials they need to realize their ideas. Planning documents can include a place for students to draw their proposed solution and another place for them to list the necessary materials. Labeling each part on a sketch encourages students to think about which materials they may need. Since planning is an iterative process, students often change their plans and consequently their materials as they manipulate them and test. Teachers need to consider whether they want students to amend their plans to include the additional materials. There is no right way to do this, and the choice usually depends on the allocated time for the project. If there is sufficient time, students could alter their plans. Another option is for students to orally explain why they have altered their plan. A third option is to include a reflection at the end of the unit asking students what they changed about their initial plans and why. Finally, teachers can use design talks, described in Chapter 10, to scaffold student thinking as they plan materials for their design.

Students have multiple ways to choose and interact with materials when engaged in engineering activities. Selected materials may change between an initial plan and the final build depending on several things including students' perception of the properties of materials, available materials, and feedback from testing and project time.

13

Assessment

Assessing engineering involves more nuance than simply grading whether a students' final project works or not. Even when students do not produce a fully functioning device, they make progress in learning engineering skills. Assessment should allow educators to document the ways in which students are making progress. We view assessment as information from students that helps both the students and educators guide learning.

Engineering work can take many forms and focus on different aspects of the discipline. Formative assessment allows us to observe students' initial understanding of materials or engineering design practices and then use the information to inform teaching practices. Summative assessment provides a final snapshot to summarize where the classroom engineering activities have taken students' engineering knowledge and practices.

Both formative and summative assessments should be closely aligned with instructional goals, which vary widely within engineering activities. For instance, educators may prioritize the development of students' engineering practices and aim to assess their progress toward following these practices. In a science context, the goals might center on students' comprehension of scientific phenomena as applied through engineering principles. Additionally, many teachers leverage engineering activities to cultivate students' collaboration and critical thinking abilities.

DOI: 10.4324/9781003378174-13

Formative Assessment

Formative assessment allows educators to monitor students' progress and understanding during an engineering activity so they can adjust instruction or practices as needed. Students approach engineering activities with a wide variety of experiences with materials, group work, and motor skills, and it's important to understand where each student is when they begin an activity. There are many moments during an engineering activity when formative assessment can play a role. Next we describe an example from one classroom doing a Chair for a Bear activity during which the teacher includes multiple formative assessment strategies.

Initial Projects

A low-stakes launching activity such as Chair for a Bear helps teachers better understand students' skills and knowledge. (See Appendix N for a Chair for a Bear lesson plan.) Launching activities also guides us as to the types of classroom discussions and support needed. In the following example from a first-grade classroom, the teacher, Deb, uses several techniques to assess her students' understanding and work.

Deb's first-grade class built a chair for a teddy bear out of craft materials. They had cardboard tubes, popsicle sticks, boxes (recycled cereal and tissues), plastic containers (yogurt), construction paper, masking tape, and glue sticks. Deb placed the students in pairs to work on the design challenge. She asked each student to draw their idea on a piece of paper before they started building so students would talk to their partner about their design ideas.

As she visited each pair while they planned, she checked to see if they both agreed on the materials to use and how to attach them. A few pairs needed support talking to each other, so she prompted one partner, "Elyse, can you tell me your idea?" and gave the other the following prompt: "Chadley, what was Elyse's idea? How would you want to change or add on to her idea?" These prompts supported the students in coming up with a single shared idea and artifact.

At Asher and Austin's table, Deb listened to them explain their drawing and supported them by labeling the materials for them on their drawing, so they had a written representation to remember what materials they chose. At another table, Chris and Ethan proposed a very tall chair that appeared to be on tiny legs. She asked them to talk about the planned chair and explain what materials they would use to make the chair. Chris said, "Safety pins!" and giggled. Deb reminded them about the materials available and how they could build the chair with those materials. They mentioned popsicle sticks but noted they might be difficult to build with: "Those will be hard to balance," says Ethan. The partners finally agreed that straws might work.

Observations and Questions

Deb's most fundamental tools are observation and questions. As she visited groups, she looked for ways in which the students participated in the activity. Her first-grade students were learning to collaborate, so when she saw them working more individually, she served as an intermediary to help them work together. She asked questions and reminded the students to listen to each other's ideas, saying "Chadley, what is Elyse's idea?" as she guided them toward collaboratively building a single chair.

Drawing as Planning

Drawings can be a useful tool for students to share ideas. Looking at students' drawings' can help teachers see what the students intend to build and help scaffold their building process. Deb helped Asher and Austin label the materials they planned to use so they would remember their ideas when they selected materials from the table on the side of the classroom. When she viewed Chris and Ethan's drawing, she noticed that their design was likely going to be hard to build. The drawing helps her talk to the pair about their building materials, guiding them to use what was available. In both cases, Deb first listened to the students to figure out what they aimed to do and then built upon those ideas, helping them collaborate or narrow their focus.

This initial project helped Deb establish norms and identify her students' needs. After doing the Chair for a Bear activity, she led a discussion where the class discussed how the partner teams combined their ideas. They wrote down a list of things partners do to share ideas.

Things We Do to Be a Good Partner

1) We listen to our partner's ideas like detectives.
2) We agree to include ideas from both partners in the design.
3) We try both ideas to figure out what works.
4) We both get time to build.
5) We take breaks when we are frustrated or mad.

They also looked at some of the drawings to talk about what aspects had helped them build (Figure 13.1). They talked about how it was helpful to label the materials and draw what the materials looked like. One student

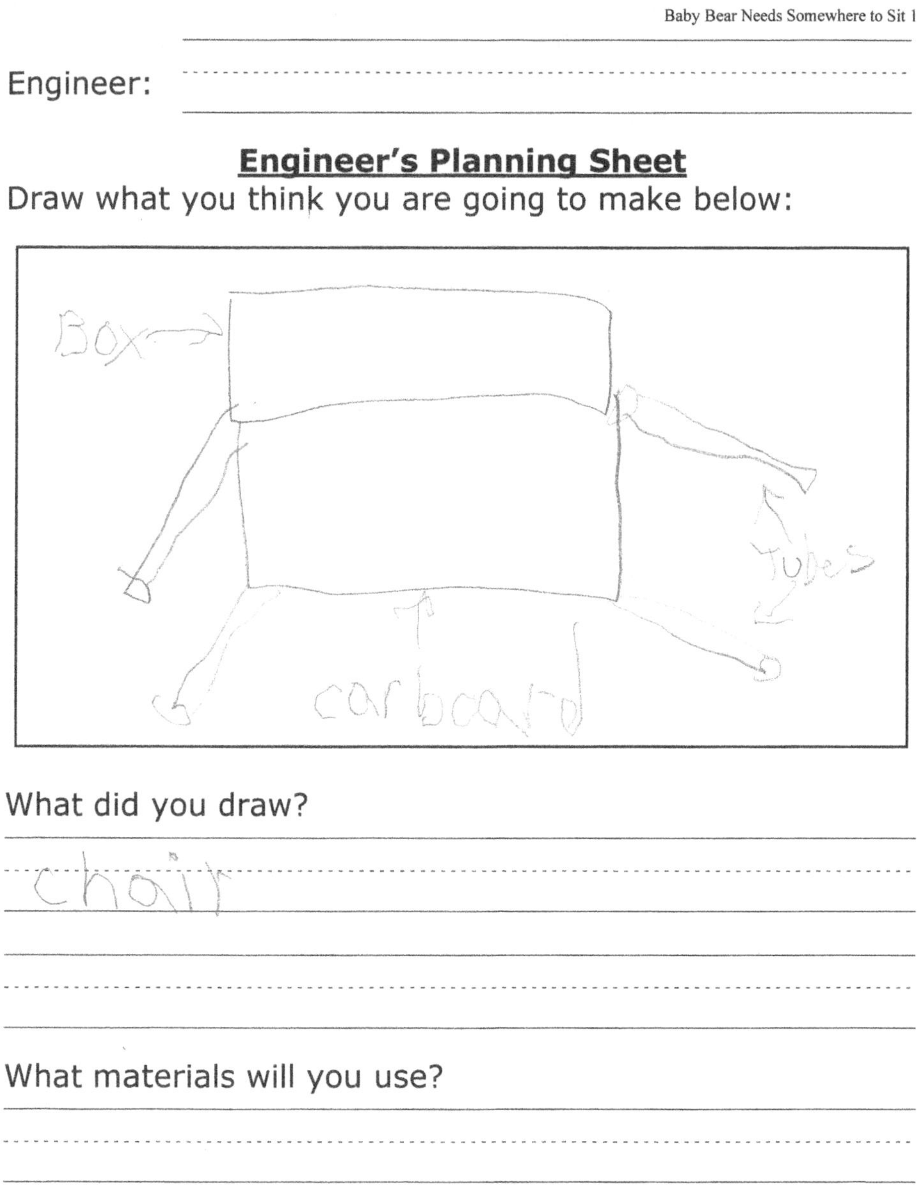

Baby Bear Needs Somewhere to Sit 1

Engineer: _____

Engineer's Planning Sheet

Draw what you think you are going to make below:

What did you draw?

chair

What materials will you use?

Figure 13.1 Two student planning drawings.

highlighted how it was good to have a drawing so both partners agreed on what they were building.

Next, we can also look at formative assessment in an initial project from an upper grade. One of Amina's sixth-grade STEM classes is using robotics kits for the first time. She meets with students for four 45-minute sessions each week. In the first week, she has students do an activity called

Silly Walks. (See Appendix V for the Silly Walks lesson plan.) The activity requires students to make their robots move without rolling on wheels. The project also requires that the motors and assorted pieces attach to the main brick so the whole robot moves. Amina chose the project for its multiple possible solutions, allowing students to explore the materials freely without worry.

Baby Bear Needs Somewhere to Sit 1

Engineer: _____

Engineer's Planning Sheet
Draw what you think you are going to make below:

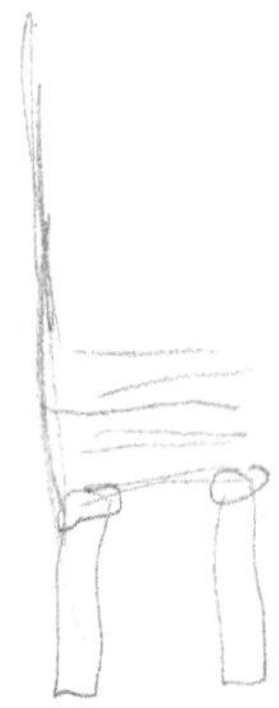

What did you draw?

chair and legs

What materials will you use?

Figure 13.1 (Continued)

She anticipates that her students will have different levels of experience with the robotic kit pieces. In groups of two or three, the students have ten minutes to come up with their first idea for attaching pieces just to the motor. Walking around the room, she notices students with less experience needing some support. At the ten-minute mark, all the groups share their ideas. As groups share, she points out building techniques that may help groups use a larger variety of pieces. She takes pictures of the designs and puts them in an online slide deck that students can refer to for inspiration.

Groups then go on to build their silly walk robots over the next two class periods. A few groups have trouble connecting the motors to the main brick that provides the power to move the whole robot. Amina encourages groups to visit other groups for inspiration. Many groups succeed, but one or two are still struggling. She wraps up each class period by updating the online slide deck to illustrate how some groups have connected their designs. The deck serves as a resource to support students who are still connecting motors to the main brick. Like Deb, Amina consistently observes her students to assess their progress with robotic building. She uses these ongoing observations to provide scaffolds and instructional support for students to advance their own creative insights.

Engineering Notebooks

While observations are useful, it can be challenging to spend time with each group in a busy classroom. Moreover, some parts of engineering design are less visible than others. Engineering notebooks offer an efficient way to support formative assessment. These documents, either physical or digital, follow many formats to help students document and reflect on their engineering design practices. Engineering notebooks provide a structure for students to capture their ideas and iterations. Some educators simply use paper notebooks and have students respond to a prompt.

In the example in Figure 13.2, the fourth-grade teacher asked the class to reflect on their progress in building a tower of plastic cups and card stock. The students wrote about how they tested and rebuilt the towers to make them stable. The notebook content helped the teacher craft feedback on the students' engineering practice. She commends them on testing their idea to make sure it worked.

Marcus is a middle school engineering and technology teacher. He has students do a range of engineering projects from simple cardboard towers to complex arcade games using 3D printers. He uses a digital engineering notebook, Design Cards, in Google Slides. Each group of students has a template of cards that prompt them to document aspects of the engineering design process. There are six types of slides (problem, exploration, ideas, test, feature,

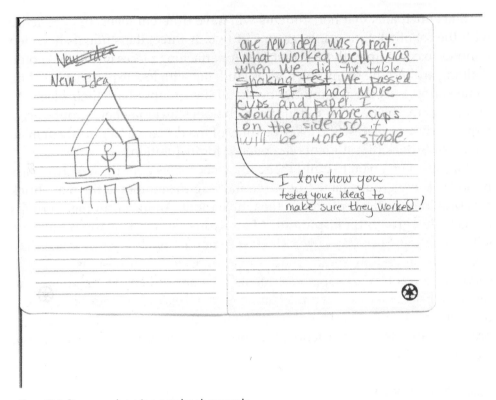

Figure 13.2 Paper engineering notebook example.

and final design) (see Figure 13.3).[1] Each day as students work on their project, they document their work on these cards/slides.

For example, a group working on a game might first use a problem card to document the arcade game they are going to work on. They might do some research online and document the types of games they found on an exploration slide. Students use the Idea slide to plan their design and use the test slide to document the results physical prototype testing. Groups can use an issue slide to document a problem they want help with. To document their final design, they have feature and final design slides. Groups can use as many slides as they want and in any order.

While Marcus moved around the classroom, he visited each group, reviewing their design cards to get valuable formative feedback on their progress. Some days he used only the test cards as he met with individual groups. For example, after working on arcade challenges, he looked at each of the groups' test cards to see how they were progressing toward getting different features of their designs to work. A few of the groups had trouble with launching a ball to create a pinball-like game. At the beginning of the next class, he led a discussion about different materials and mechanisms that could be used to move a small ball.

PROBLEM

Record what you try and do and discover to improve your design.

Criteria	How will you test it?
Constraints	Draw the test

EXPLORATION

Record what you try and do and discover to improve your design.

Sketch what you tried	Sketch what you tried
Add test results or notes	Add test results or notes

IDEAS

Describe multiple ideas or different aspects of an idea.

Sketch an idea	Sketch an idea
Add description, materials, etc.	

Figure 13.3 Design cards used for digital and physical engineering notebook.

TEST

Complete one test card for every test.

	What did you change?
	What was the test result?
	Any ideas why?

FEATURE

Describe a cool part of your design to share with others, even if it failed.

Sketch a feature	Description
	Function
	Pros and cons

FINAL DESIGN

Describe your final solution and what you would do with more time.

Sketch the final design

Add description, materials, etc.

Figure 13.3 (Continued)

Summative Assessment

Assessing engineering work to produce a final evaluation or grade is challenging as we are looking to assess the learning that happened. While an important component of professional engineering is whether a design is fully functional, in educational settings, we want to know more about what the student learned and how they are developing engineering practices.

Beyond the Final Artifact

Many teachers involved in engineering design have observed the power of the hands-on component of engineering design projects, and students can have a meaningful learning experience even if their final design presents functional or construction issues. In other words, the final constructed artifact does not represent all the learning that has happened. Many factors beyond a student's control can impact final functionality such as fine motor skills, absences (limiting time), or insufficient materials in the classroom. We want to think about summative assessment holistically so we can capture what students have done throughout a design activity. Documentation tools can provide opportunities for students to reflect on and synthesize their experiences while also creating evidence for a summative assessment.

Tools for Documentation

Engineering Notebooks

Paper or digital notebooks can also be used for summative assessment. Similar to formative assessment, one way to assess students' final progress is to encourage students to document their work as they progress. Engineering notebooks are useful tools for students to capture pictures and drawings of their prototypes as well as record changes between iterations. Used in a summative nature, slides or pages from an engineering notebook can be used for students to present a narrative of the different engineering design practices used throughout an activity. A record of these practices will often illustrate growth.

Reflection Prompts

Reflection prompts can help students to capture and interpret how they engaged in the engineering activity. Including reflection topics in early project discussions helps students think about the relevant issues as they progress.

The format of reflection prompts should reflect the needs of the students and goals of the teacher. Table 13.1 outlines example prompts and goals. Writing is one option, but it may not be the most accessible format for all learners and may not fully capture what they have learned. Teachers may need to

Table 13.1 Sample Reflection Prompts

Prompt	Goal
Tell me about one problem you found with your design when you tested it and how you changed your design to fix it.	Capture what students notice about their design's performance and how they can connect that to changes they made.
Describe how you and your partner decided on your design.	Capture how students collaborated and compromised on ideas.
Share how you would modify your design if you had additional time and materials.	Capture how students understand their design and how it can be improved.
Discuss the strengths and weaknesses of your final design.	Capture students' ability to analyze the strengths and weaknesses of their design.

record answers for their younger students. Multilingual students benefit from having options to respond in ways that work best for them. Some teachers find audio or video formats effective in capturing capture students' thinking.

Portfolios

Portfolios are often used in engineering for summative assessment. A portfolio summarizes the project with photos and descriptions. In engineering, it's helpful to have pictures of the design as well as of the tools used to create the solution, such as code and CAD models. In addition to an assessment tool, students' curation of their portfolio can be a chance for reflection. Portfolios can be completed physically, electronically, or both.

Rubrics

Rubrics are also valuable tools for summative assessment. Effective engineering project rubrics match learning goals and provide students with criteria on how their teacher will look at their work. Educators emphasize process and product in different ways depending on their goals. In this section, we'll look at Ryan and Silvia, who have different approaches to final assessment.

Ryan is a middle school STEM teacher. He uses an engineering rubric focused on practices for many different projects. See Table 13.2. His class emphasizes all the engineering practices, and the rubric helps him to document evidence of both student engagement in these practices and group collaboration. The rubric includes all elements of the engineering design process such as

Table 13.2 Middle School Engineering Rubric (also in Appendix D)

Element	Criteria
PROBLEM	• Problem is stated clearly in the student's own words. • Criteria and constraints are identified.
RESEARCH	• Three facts are identified from research that will assist in design. • Student explains how those facts would assist in their planning and construction.
BRAINSTORM	• Three or more unique ideas are produced. • Each plan has a simple explanation of how it works.
PLAN	• A detailed sketch includes a solution. • There are at least two different viewing angles (front, side, top, bottom). • Key parts are labeled and explained. • There is a rough estimate of the materials and amount. • There is an explanation of how the solution works (3–4 sentences).
CONSTRUCTION	• The building log has daily pictures of the project as well as goals for each building day. • Materials are handled with care and respect. • Everyone equally contributed to the design, and all ideas were respected. • Rules and guidelines were followed.
TEST/REDESIGN	• Tests follow the criteria and constraints. • Students can identify successes and problems from each test. • Students address problems and improve design before the next test. • If students feel that they have been successful and no further testing is needed, they can clearly explain why they were successful.
COMMUNICATE	**Each section of the student's building journal is complete, including answers to the following questions.** • Do you think you were successful in this challenge? Why or why not? • If you were to do this challenge again, explain what you would do differently. • What advice would you give students who were going to attempt this project next time?

Overall Grade—Engineering Design Process		
Developing	**Progressing**	**Meeting Standard**
Fewer than 11 of the criteria were met/ Journal was not turned in	12–18 of the criteria were met	19 All the criteria were met

finding the problem, conducting research, and planning their design. Including all the design process elements conveys that all phases are equally important.

While Ryan focused more on the practices of engineering, Silvia, also a middle school STEM educator, was interested in a balance of engineering practices as well as the final product. Silvia used the rubric illustrated in Table 13.3 to support a specific project where students created a robotic solution to a problem in the book *The Giver* by L. Lowry. The rubric reflects the mix of the instructional goals that she wanted to evaluate. She had four key areas that she wanted to assess. Part 1 looks at how students considered the story in planning their design. Parts 2 and 3 focus on the technical aspects of building and programming the robot. Part 4 looks at communication and documentation.

In this chapter, we have discussed tools to support formative and summative assessment in engineering teaching and learning. Assessment is an integral part of engineering teaching and learning, providing teachers insight into where to focus and how students are developing engineering practices and proficiency with tools through activities. Assessment tools should support teachers' instructional goals for their students as well as help students reflect on their own learning.

Table 13.3 Sample Engineering Design and Robotics Rubric (also in Appendix E)

PART 1 PLANNING AND CREATIVITY (30 POSSIBLE POINTS)		
Category	**Possible Points**	**Earned Points**
Character selection and justification *Is the chosen character relevant and well explained?*	5	
Object selection and justification *Is the chosen object relevant and meaningful for the character?*	5	
Character's transportation needs and motivation *Are the reasons for transporting the object clear and well developed?*	5	

Start and end points of transportation *Are the locations clear and relevant to the character?*	5	
Paragraph, clarity, grammar, and flow *Is the paragraph well written, free of errors, and engaging?*	5	
Originality and creativity in the transportation concept *Does the transportation device incorporate unique and interesting ideas?*	5	
Total Part 1	30	

PART 2 TRANSPORT DESIGN AND CONSTRUCTION (30 POSSIBLE POINTS)		
Category	**Value**	**Points**
Functionality of the transport device *Does the device successfully transport the object?*	15	
Design and attachment to root robot *Is the device creative, functional, and securely attached to the robot?*	10	
Use of materials and craftsmanship *Are the materials appropriate and used skillfully?*	5	
Total Part 2	30	

PART 3 PROGRAMMING AND TESTING (20 POSSIBLE POINTS)		
Programming accuracy and functionality *Does the program successfully navigate the robot from point A to point B?*	10	
Code efficiency and clarity *Is the code well written, organized, and easy to understand?*	5	
Demonstration and successful transport *Does the robot reliably travel the intended path without deviation?*	5	
Total Part 3	20	

PART 4 PHOTOS AND VIDEO PRESENTATIONS (20 POSSIBLE POINTS)		
Clarity and relevance of photos *Do the photos clearly show the transport device and functionality?*	10	
Video clarity and demonstration *Does the video clearly show the robot successfully transporting the object?*	10	
Total Part 4	20	
Total Score	**100**	

Note

1 These slides can also be printed from introducingengineering.org.

Reference

Lowry, L. (1993). *The giver*. Boston, MA: Houghton Mifflin.

14

Engineering Design Activity Sequences

The long-term objective of engaging in engineering activities is for students to work on open-ended engineering design problems that give them rich experiences as problem solvers. However, before choosing their own problems, students need the foundational skills and knowledge to use the materials effectively, and productively navigate through the engineering design process. In this chapter, we address activity sequences with open-ended projects that allow students to use a broad range of engineering skills and connect to topics they find interesting. We will also share a tool that can be used for planning engineering activities or to assess existing activities.

Engineering looks different in every classroom, with teachers paying attention to different parts of the process. Two classes may do the same activity, but the activity may occur in a different place in the class's sequence of engineering activities. In addition, one class may have more time for iteration, while another may focus on planning or problem scoping. The sequences do not need to be implemented in the same order as they are presented. Readers are encouraged to select activities and sequences that work for their classrooms.

As discussed previously, engineers do many things as they move through the process and design, but students do not need to engage in every engineering practice during each activity. In the sequences we share, we begin with more structured activities that can be classified as skill builders. These introductory activities focus on specific aspects of the engineering design process. An example of this type of activity is the wind tube that promotes iteration and testing.

DOI: 10.4324/9781003378174-14

When students progress through each sequence of activities, the individual activities become less structured, encouraging independence and initiative. In general, most final activities for the sequences are very open-ended. Students not only engage in each of the engineering skills but also manage the time and the elements of the design process. The Guminator is an excellent example of an open-ended activity where students demonstrated agency and initiative in responding to the prompt, "make something to improve the school."

We acknowledge that time is a constraint and that not everyone has time to do larger projects. If this is the case, pick activities that meet the class's goals and with which students can succeed. The activities in the sequences have been conducted with students in kindergarten to high school. Of course, younger students will need more time than older students. In the following sequences, each session is sixty minutes. Lesson plans for the individual activities are included in the Appendices. The assumption for all sequences is that classes have discussed engineering and norms before lessons 1.

Sequence 1

The first sequence in Table 14.1 uses recycled and craft materials and builds toward a very open-ended design project. This activity starts with a simple activity, Wind Tube, with given constraints and requirements. As the sequence progresses, students interact with more materials and have more opportunities to explore multiple solutions. They also explore how to consider clients' needs when engineering a solution. The sequence culminates with an in-depth project that requires students to identify a problem in their school, scope the problem determining criteria and constraints, plan and prototype a working design, and get feedback from testing their design on the real problem.

Sequence 2

Like Sequence 1, Sequence 2 in Table 14.2 uses recycled and craft materials. However, this sequence builds more knowledge of materials and mechanisms than Sequence 1, laying a strong foundation for the final project.

Table 14.1 Activity Sequence 1

Days	Activity	Goal
1	Wind Tube	Introduce engineering, iteration, testing, and failure
2-3	Stomp Rocket	Build collective knowledge, supporting literacy practices, evaluation, and communication
4	Pencil Holder	Explore materials, work within constraints, collaborate
5-6	Backpack	Design for a client, develop constraints and criteria, test and iterate
7-9	Abby the Dog	Research, design for a client, work within constraints
10-13	Novel Engineering: Peter's Chair	Identify and scope problems *Read the book at the beginning of the session.
14-20	Final Project: Improve your Classroom/School Intro & Problem Scope	Manage the full engineering design process

Table 14.2 Activity Sequence 2

Days	Activity	Goal
1	Product Comparison	Identify and balance criteria
2	Pencil Holder	Explore materials, work with constraints, collaborate
3-4	Build a House	Explore materials
5	Crane System	Design and build simple machines, test and explore systems engineering
6	Exploring Circuits (lights, buzzers, & batteries)	Explore circuits
7	Lunchbox Alarm	Design including circuits
8-9	Chair for a Bear	Design for criteria and constraints, test
10-13	Abby the Dog	Scope problems, identify criteria and constraints
14-20	Final Project: Game for a Younger Student	Manage the full engineering design process

Table 14.3 Activity Sequence 3

Days	Activity	Goal
1	Back Scratcher	Explore materials, test
2-3	Chair for a Bear	Build sturdy designs, think about a client
4	Silly Walks	Introduce robotics and motors
5-6	Artbot	Introduce programming and gears
7-8	Lunchbox Alarm	Introduce sensors
9-10	Biomimicry: Digging	Put it all together: mechanisms and programming
11-13	Mini Golf	Build more complex systems
14-20	Final Project: Amusement Park Ride	Manage the full engineering design process

Sequence 3: Robotics

The sequence in Table 14.3 uses robotics materials. Like Sequence 2, these activities give students experience with engineering design and the necessary materials. In robotics, regardless of the toolkit used, students typically learn how to use the building kit to construct sturdy structures, integrate motors for motions, and employ sensors and programming to create responsive design. Many students have not had access to these types of materials, so letting them develop comfort and proficiency with the robotics materials is important. If students seem apprehensive about materials, it is useful to add another activity or even a choice build (build something that moves that is triggered by a sensor) to the sequence to build their confidence.

Final Project Trajectory

In these sequences, final activities are open-ended, allowing for students to choose their own problems. Hence, there are no lesson plans for the final project. As a note, students may not follow this flow exactly. For example, some students may begin brainstorming during Day 1 or spend time beyond Day 1 problem scoping. Table 14.4 outlines a possible trajectory of a final project sequence.

These sequences are simply examples of possible trajectories. After facilitating a few activities with students, teachers often gain confidence in designing their own activities. These activities can also achieve the same goals.

Table 14.4 Activity Sequence 4: Final Project/Longer Project Trajectory

Day	Sub-Activity	Notes
1	Introduce Challenge and Problem Scoping	Students begin filling in their planning document as they scope the problem.
2	Research, Brainstorm, Planning	Students continue to fill in the planning worksheet, manipulating materials as needed.
3	Build	Students test as they build. These may be mini tests of components or tests to see how their designs work overall. Students will iterate as they test and document as they work.
4	Mid-Design Share-out & Building	Students continue to test, iterate, and document.
5	Build	Students continue to test, iterate, and document.
6	Final Share-Out	Students share across groups or with whole class.
7	Clean-up and Reflection	Reflection may be part of documentation and/or class discussion. It can include personal reflections on the process and/or lessons learned about topics such as materials and collaboration.

Planning Documents

The engineering design framework that we have presented throughout the book is a useful tool for planning and assessing existing activities. The Classroom Engineering Activity is a full planner that guides teachers as they plan activities for their classrooms and anticipates how students may respond. Next, we give an overview of the planner, and the full planner is included in the Appendices.

Before exploring the planning document, the Classroom Engineering Activity, readers may want to review other parts of the book that dealt with activity planning and design. Chapter 6 of the book details activity planning. When planning, the first step is to consider both the engineering goals and goals associated with other disciplines. The next step is to think about the students' experiences and which foundational skills they may still need to practice. Fostering student agency remains a central goal; however, students need to understand the expectations and know how to navigate the engineering design process. Chapter 11 offers suggestions on inclusive engineering activity design.

Use the Classroom Engineering Activity overview to consider the following questions when planning an activity.

Challenge/Problem

Pick a problem or context that lends itself to engineering solutions. **See Chapter 5 for more details on what makes an engineering problem.**

> *Will students pick a problem, or will you tell them what the problem/challenge is?*
>
> *Are the multiple problems that could be identified by the groups?*
>
> *Will there be a client or something to help?*

Introduction

Think about how to introduce the problem and the resources students need to succeed.

> *Do students have prior knowledge of or experience with the topic?*
>
> *How will students connect the topic to things they are familiar with?*
>
> *How will students gain an understanding of the client(s) and stakeholder(s), if there are any?*

Goals

What are the goals for the activity and how will you communicate them to your students?

> *Reading, writing, and oral communication can also address ELA goals.*
>
> *How will you communicate your goals to your students?*

Cross-Curricular Connections

Will the activity connect to disciplines other than engineering and what are the goals for these connections?

> *How will you make connections to other subjects?*
>
> *What are the goals for these connections?*

Classroom Management

What is the best way to group students and help them manage their work?

> *Will the entire class work on the same problem or multiple problems?*
>
> *How will the students plan?*
>
> *Will you provide students with a planning document?*

Materials

As you think about the problems and possible solutions, think about which materials students will need. **See Chapter 12 for more details on materials.**

> *Where will you store materials?*
>
> *How will you allocate materials?*
>
> *Depending on their experience, how will you allocate time students need to play or experiment with materials?*
>
> *Will you give all students or groups the same materials, or can they choose?*

Discussions

Pick points in the process where you will facilitate discussion. Think about which types of conversations will leave students with the most information as they move forward. **See Chapter 10 for more details on discussions and design talks.**

> *Which type of design talk might you incorporate and when?*
>
> *What behaviors can you model for students?*

Feedback, Evaluation, and Testing

How will feedback be managed?

> *How will you provide space and time for the testing of designs?*
>
> *Will you provide students with testing sheets?*
>
> *Will you model peer feedback?*

Engineering

For each phase of the engineering design process, consider how to best support students and what resources they will need.

> *Will the students name the design criteria? Will you provide the criteria? Will it be a combination?*
>
> *Will students have time to do research? Will you provide background information? Will it be a combination of the two?*
>
> *How will you help students consider multiple solutions?*
>
> *How will you help students work toward functional designs?*
>
> *Will students produce an artifact they build, a conceptual plan, a system?*
>
> *How will students know if a design or solution is successful?*

Assessment

What will formative and summative assessment look like? **See Chapter 13 for more details on assessment**.

> *What evidence or work will you look at for assessment?*
>
> *What formats will you include for assessment?*

Timeline

Given the goals and scope of the activity, how much time will the activity take?

> *Will you allow more time if students do not finish on time?*

Conclusion

Planning for an introductory activity or planning an entire sequence involves thinking about your goals for your students and then working backward to figure out where to begin. Start at a place that is comfortable for you. Some teachers prefer starting slowly with a short activity that is discussion-based. Others may be ready to jump in a little deeper with a building activity. The planning materials included in this book will help you think about what engineering will look like in your classroom.

With each activity, you will become more familiar with engineering and what your students will do as they engineer. In time, you will better anticipate what your students will do and plan according to these anticipated behaviors. Additionally, your students will better understand what is expected of them as they engineer, and they will move through the engineering design process more independently.

Bringing engineering to the K-8 classroom means you, as an educator, are giving students access to a powerful way of thinking and learning. Beyond the required standards, engineering gives students a set of practices to tackle problems they see in the world, today and in the future. Looking to the future, we want ALL students to know that engineering can be a potential pathway by making relevant connections between the discipline of engineering, their lives, and their strengths.

Appendices

Classroom Resources
    A. Student Planning Sheet
    B. Student Testing Sheet
    C. Teacher Activity Planner
    D. Assessment Rubric: Engineering Activity Checklist
    E. Assessment Matrix
    F. Materials Request from Home Template Letter

Lesson Plans
    G. Product Comparison
    H. Pencil Holder
    I.   Wind Tube
    J.   Wind Tube Building Directions
    K. Backpack for a Stuffed Animal
    L. Create a System to Lift a Weight onto a Chair
    M. Build a House
    N. Chair for a Bear
    O. Stomp Rocket
    P. Novel Engineering: Peter's Chair
    Q. Abby the Dog
    R. Back Scratcher
    S. Exploring Circuits
    T. Art Bot
    U. Miniature Golf Course
    V. Silly Walks
    W. Biomimetics
    X. Lunchbox Protector
    Y. Longer/Final Project Trajectory

Supporting Content
    Z. Related Websites

Classroom Resources

Appendix A
Student Planning Sheet

Your Name & Your Partner: _____

Who is your client? _____

Is there anything special you need to think about for your client?

_____

_____

_____

Draw your design.

What materials will you use?

Reflection

What did you notice when you tested your design?	
What worked well?	
What needs to be improved?	

Appendix B
Student Testing Sheet

Draw your current design:

What did you **change** about your design from your last test?

What was the test **result**?
(Did it pass the test? Fail? Partially pass?)

Any ideas **why** your design performed like that in the test?

Appendix C

Teacher Activity Planner

Name of Activity	Think About . . .
Challenge/Problem	
What is the challenge? Is it engineering? • The activity has a goal or problem with criteria and constraints for which students are creating a solution. • Students can create more than one solution to this problem. • Students' solutions are testable and can inform future iterations; they can get feedback from clients/peers or by using their solution in the real world to evaluate it.	• Will students pick a problem or will you tell them what the problem/ challenge is? • Are there multiple problems that could be identified by groups? • Will there be a client or another form of help?
Introduction	
How will you introduce the activity? What resources will you use?	• Do students have prior knowledge/ experience with the topic? • Can you make connections to things that students are familiar with? • How will students gain an understanding of the client(s) and stakeholders(s), if there are any?
Goals	
What are your goals for the activity? What standards will you address?	• Reading, writing, and oral communication can also address English language arts goals. • How will you communicate these goals?
Cross-Curricular Connection	
In addition to engineering, are there other subjects that connect to the activity?	• How will you make connections to other subjects? • What are your goals for these connections?

Classroom Management	
How will students be grouped? How will you support students to document? Will worksheets be needed? What other supports will you use for students? What difficulties do you anticipate students having?	• Will the entire class work on the same problem or multiple problems? • How will students plan? • Will you provide students with a planning document?
Materials	
What materials will be available to students? How and when will you introduce students to materials?	• Where will you store materials? • How will you allocate materials? • Depending on their experience, students may need time to play or experiment with materials. • Will you give all students/groups the same materials or can they choose?
Discussions	
At what points in the process will you have structured discussions? What kinds of discussions do you anticipate that would encourage you to facilitate impromptu discussions? How will you support students to have productive group discussions?	• Which type of design talk might you incorporate and when? • What behaviors can you model for students? How will you provide space and time for testing designs? • Will you provide students with testing sheets? • What are the implications of your solution and/or who or what will be impacted?
Feedback, Evaluation, & Testing	
Will you have a testing station or will there need to be multiple ways to test ideas? Will you incorporate peer feedback sessions?	• Will you require students to all test at the same time? • Will you model peer feedback? • How will you describe testing protocols to students?
Engineering	
Problem-Scoping What constraints will you impose, if any? How will you model communication of design ideas and constraints?	• Will students name the design criteria, will you give them the criteria, or will it be a combination?

Research prior solution/client What prior knowledge will students need to engage in the design problem?	• Will students be given time to do research, and will you provide background information, or will it be a combination of the two?
Planning How much focus will be on planning? Will students submit a short plan or will they complete a detailed plan?	• How will you help students consider multiple solutions? • How will you help students work toward functional designs? • When will it be appropriate to have a model vs. a conceptual plan vs. a functional model?
Creating What will students produce? An artifact they build, a conceptual plan, a system?	• How much time will they spend building/creating related to the other design steps?
Evaluating How will you help students think about successful design and consider meeting design criteria? How will you help students think about how they are engaging in the design process?	• How will students know if a design/solution is successful? • How will you help students analyze their designs to assess what is working well and what can be improved?
Time to Iterate and Reflect How will you support students to reflect on their process? How will you talk to students about the role of iteration throughout the design process? How will you support students to iterate on their ideas and designs?	• How will students document their process? • Will there be whole-class discussion to support iteration and reflection or will students' documentation lead students to reflect and iterate?
Assessment	
How will you assess students? What tools will you use for formative and summative assessment? What type(s) of documentation will students need to complete?	• Will you assess individuals or groups? • What evidence/work will you look at? • Which standards will you assess (engineering, science, writing, group work, etc.)?

Timeline	
How much time do you have for the activity?	Elements to Plan for • introduction • design talks • constraints criteria • planning • introducing materials • building and testing • mid-design sharing • redesigning • final sharing • evaluating/assessing

Appendix D
Assessment Rubric: Engineering Activity Checklist

Student Name:
Project:

Element	Criteria
Problem	• Problem is stated clearly in the student's own words. • Criteria and constraints are identified.
Research	• Three facts are identified from research that will assist in design. • Student explains how those facts would assist in their planning/construction.
Brainstorm	• Three or more unique ideas are presented. • Each plan has a simple explanation on how it works.
Plan	A detailed sketch is made of a solution including • at least two different viewing angles (front, side, top, bottom). • key parts labeled and explained. • a rough estimate of materials and amount. • an explanation of how the solution works (3-4 sentences).
Construction	• Building log has daily pictures of project as well as goals for each building day. • Materials are handled with care and respect. • Everyone equally contributed to the design, and all ideas were respected. • Students follow the teacher's rules and guidelines.
Test/Redesign	• Students conduct tests following the criteria and constraints. • Students are able to identify successes and problems from each test. • Students address problems and improve design before the next test. • If students feel that they have been successful and no further testing is needed, they can clearly explain why they were successful.

Communicate	Each section of the student's building journal is complete, including answers to the following questions: • Do you think you were successful in this challenge? Why or why not? • If you were to do this challenge again, explain what you would do differently? • What advice would you give students who were going to attempt this project next time?
Notes/Feedback	

Overall Grade			
Standard	Developing/Not Yet	Progressing	Meeting
Engineering Design Process	Less than 11 of the criteria were met/ Journal was not turned in	12–18 of criteria were met	19 All of the criteria were met

Appendix E

Assessment Matrix

Part 1: Planning and Creativity (30 possible points)		
Character selection and justification (5 points)		Is the chosen character relevant and well explained?
Object selection and justification (5 points)		Is the chosen object relevant and meaningful for the character?
Character's transportation needs and motivation (5 points)		Are the reasons for transporting the object clear and well developed?
Start and end points of transportation (5 points)		Are the locations clear and relevant to the character?
Paragraph, clarity, grammar, and flow (5 points)		Is the paragraph well written, free of errors, and engaging?
Originality and creativity in the transportation concept (5 points)		Does the transportation device incorporate unique and interesting ideas?
Total Part 1	30	
Part 2: Transport Design and Construction (30 possible points)		
Functionality of the transport device (15 points)		Does the device successfully transport the object?
Design and attached to root robot (10 points)		Is the device creative, functional, and securely attached to the robot?
Use of materials and craftsmanship (5 points)		Are the materials appropriate and used skillfully?
Total Part 2	30	

Part 3: Programming and Testing (20 possible points)		
Programming accuracy and functionality (10 points)		Does the program successfully navigate the robot from point A to point B?
Code efficiency and clarity (5 points)		Is the code well-written, organized, and easy to understand?
Demonstration and successful transport (5 points)		Does the robot reliably travel the intended path without deviation?
Total Part 3	20	
Part 4: Photos and Video Presentations (20 possible points)		
Clarity and relevance of photos (10 points)		Do the photos clearly show the transport device and functionality?
Video clarity and demonstration (10 points)		Does the video clearly show the robot successfully transporting the object?
Total Part 4	20	
Total Score	100	

Appendix F

Materials Request from Home Template Letter

Dear Families,

This year, our classroom will be doing engineering design activities. The students will be guided as they build things to solve engineering problems. To do this, we will use a variety of materials. Materials will include craft and recyclable materials. Listed below are some of the items we will need. If you would like to contribute to our collection, please send any of the listed materials to school with your child. Please do not buy materials, but only donate what you have around the house.

- duct tape
- plastic straws
- paper clips
- fishing line
- paper cups
- empty cereal boxes
- plastic food containers (if used, please make sure they are rinsed well)
- empty tissue/shoe boxes
- empty paper towel rolls

We are very excited to do these engineering projects. I'm sure you'll hear more about them in the future.

Sincerely,

Lesson Plans

Lesson Plans

Appendix G
Product Comparison

Lesson Overview: Groups of students will compare four types of the same product and pick the best choice. Before the group work, as a class, the students will come up with a list of design features. Each small group of students will talk about the products and compare the different features, weighing the pros and cons of each item and then picking the best one. This can be expanded by giving students a specific user to think about.

Suggested Time: 45–60 minutes depending on age

Learning Objectives:
- to gain practice collaborating with a partners
- to gain an understanding of constraints and criteria
- to understand that there is not one "correct" answer

Materials: Four of one type of object that students are familiar with (pens, pencils, notebooks, water bottles, etc.)

Criteria:
- Students must pick which one of the objects they think is the best. They can pick for a specific user (pencil for a first-grader vs. teacher) or situation (water bottle for a classroom desk or a hike).

Directions:
1) Explain to the students that they will examine four objects and then choose the best one against the criteria they have outlined.
2) Model what they will be doing with a different type of object, talk about possible criteria, and fill in a table about the object.
3) Place students in groups of three or four.
4) Students will begin by picking five criteria that they think are important as they think about the object. The teacher can provide the cost of the objects.
5) Students will examine the objects and fill in the table.
6) Each group will pick the object they think is the best. They should be able to explain their reasoning.
7) Each group will share their choice with the class and their justification.
8) The teacher may provide a specific user or situation and then facilitate a discussion with the class if the user or situation changes any of their choices.

Product Comparison

Name

Product	Criteria 1 Ex: Cost	Criteria 2	Criteria 3	Criteria 4	Criteria 5	Notes

Appendix H
Pencil Holder

Lesson Overview: Students will design something to hold the 8–12 pencils/ crayons on their desk or table.

Suggested Time: 30–60 minutes depending on age

Learning Objectives:
- to gain practice collaborating with a partner
- to better understand the properties of materials
- to gain experience testing
- to gain an understanding of constraints and criteria

Materials: A variety of materials can be used for this activity. It can serve as a materials exploration. Possible materials include interlocking building bricks (standard size and large), craft and recyclables.
- interlocking building bricks
- cardboard
- paper tubes
- popsicle sticks
- tape
- paperclips
- pencils, makers, pens, or crayons

Design Criteria:
- must hold 8–12 items
- must be sturdy enough to stay together
- one holder must be built between partners

Directions:
1) Explain to students that they will build something to hold some of the materials on their tables/desks.
2) Discuss possible constraints and criteria for the device. For example, the device should be
   a. sized to fit on the table and still allow students to work.
   b. able to hold the specified items.
3) Show the students the materials to choose from.
4) Students can sketch their initial designs. Once they have a sketch, they can begin building. As you circulate, ask students questions about certain design decisions.

5) About 15 minutes into building, bring the students together and have each group share their ideas. Ask the group for ideas for any part that is difficult to build. This step takes more time, but it helps to build the community of collaboration.

6) Students should have pens and pencils at their workspaces so they can test as they go. Lead a discussion to help them analyze and interpret their designs.

7) Have students keep iterating, encouraging them to analyze and interpret after testing.

8) Be sure to leave time to have a final discussion with the class to talk about their design processes.

Appendix I
Wind Tube

Lesson Overview: Students will build something that will hover between the top two bands for 3 to 10 seconds. It can move around between those bands but can't go out the top or fall to the bottom.

Suggested Time: 40 minutes

Learning Objectives:
- to gain experience testing and iterating
- to gain an understanding of constraints and criteria
- to foster a community of collaboration
- to gain experience dealing with frustration productively

Materials:
- scissors

Recyclable Materials:
- plastic grocery bags or small trash bags
- thin cardboard (like cereal box thickness)
- old magazines
- weights: pennies, washers, or something small that provides weight
- paper towel rolls
- empty yogurt containers
- empty water bottles
- wire hangers

Purchased Materials:
- balloons (although if offered balloons sometimes that's all children will use)
- tape (masking seems to work the best) popsicle sticks
- foil
- plastic wrap
- string
- pipe cleaners
- paper clips
- coffee filters

Directions:
1) Show the students the wind tube and explain to them that they are going to build something that will hover in the wind tube between the top two rings.

2) Show the students the materials they can choose from.
3) Tell them there is little chance the designs will work the first time and that they will be able to alter the materials as needed for their designs.
4) Since the point of this activity is for students to test and iterate often, encourage them to test often and then make changes based on their tests.
5) Have students test as they build.
6) Lead a discussion of the designs to help them analyze and interpret their designs:
   a. Did your design stay between the bands?
   b. If not, did it sink or fly out?
   c. Did your design stay together inside the tube?
   d. How can you improve your design?
7) Have students keep iterating, encouraging them to analyze and interpret after testing.
8) Leave time for a final discussion with the class to talk about their designs but also the process they used and what role testing played.

Possible Discussion Topics:
   ◆ benefits and constraints of materials or inspiration provided by materials
   ◆ group dynamics
   ◆ effect of watching other groups work
   ◆ using science: thinking explicitly about drag or more like "air pushes things"
   ◆ using an "engineering design cycle" in order vs. tinkering

Appendix J
Wind Tube Building Directions

Materials:
1) plastic sheet, about 3 feet long and at least 4 feet wide
   a) Acetate works well, about 5 millimeters thick.
2) three 14" embroidery hoops
   a) Two will work, but three makes the tube sturdier.
3) clear packaging tape
4) a large fan that can face upwards (diameter larger than 14")

Procedure:
1) Roll the plastic along the long dimension into a cylinder that fits between the embroidery hoops. Secure the embroidery hoops inside and outside the plastic.
2) Use the tape to secure the seam along the outside of the tube.
3) Place the tube on top of the upward-facing fan. Tape it if it does not stay on top of the fan.

Appendix K
Backpack for a Stuffed Animal

Lesson Overview: Students will build a backpack for a client (stuffed animal) to help them carry items.

Suggested Time: 60–90 minutes

Learning Objectives:
- to gain practice identifying constraints and criteria
- to design for a client based on the constraints and criteria

Materials:
- scissors
- tape (masking seems to work the best)
- Variety of stuffed animals that are at least 8" high. Every group does not have to have a separate stuffed animal, but there should be enough that students have enough time to measure and test their designs several times while holding the stuffed animal.
- Three items per group that will be carried in the backpacks. These can be a pen, a pencil, an eraser, or items picked by students.
- thin cardboard (like cereal box thickness)
- felt and/or fabric
- popsicle sticks
- rubber bands
- string
- pipe cleaners
- plastic or paper cups
- paper clips

Directions:
1) Explain to students that they will build something to help their client carry items.
2) Discuss possible constraints and criteria for the device. For example, the device should be:
   a. removable.
   b. comfortable.
   c. able to hold the specified items.
3) Introduce how the materials and describe how the students will get them.
4) Introduce students to the "clients."

5) Students can sketch their initial designs. Once they have a sketch, they can begin building. As you circulate, ask students questions about certain design decisions.

6) About 15 minutes into building, bring the students together and have each group share their ideas. Ask the group for ideas for any part that is difficult to build. This step takes more time, but it helps to build the community of collaboration.

7) Have them test the first or second version of their design and lead a discussion to help them analyze and interpret their designs.

8) Have students keep iterating, encouraging them to analyze and interpret after testing.

9) Be sure to leave time to have a final discussion with the class to talk about their design process.

Possible Discussions Topics:
- ◆ Does your design meet the constraints and criteria?
- ◆ Why did you decide to make this like you did?
- ◆ How would your client take the backpack off?

Appendix L
Create a System to Lift a Weight onto a Chair

Lesson Overview: Students must create a system to lift a weight (a block, a bag of coins) onto a chair. Students are not allowed to touch the weight directly when lifting it.

Suggested Time: 30–60 minutes

Learning Objectives:
- to practice navigating collaboration when building a system
- to think about how individual components interact in a system

Materials:
- cylinders (cans, paper towel rolls)
- string
- plastic bags (small)
- weights (e.g., blocks, coins, batteries)
- masking tape
- thin cardboard (e.g., cereal boxes)
- paper or plastic cups
- rubber bands
- paper clips

Directions:
1) Explain to the students that they are going to build some type of system that will move the weights onto the seat of a chair.
2) Show the students the materials they can choose from.
3) Tell them they can alter the materials as needed for their designs.
4) Students can sketch their initial designs in their engineering journals. Once they have a sketch, they can begin building.
5) Have them test the first or second version of their design and lead a discussion of the designs. This can be a whole-class discussion.
6) Have students keep iterating, encouraging them to analyze and interpret after testing.
7) Be sure to leave time to have a final discussion with the class to talk about their design, but also the process they used and what role testing played.

Possible Discussion Topic:
- How did you manage building different parts in your group?
- Did other groups' ideas help you think about what you wanted to do?

Appendix M
Build a House

Lesson Overview: Students will build a house that is able to withstand the wind and rain.

Suggested Time: 60–75 minutes

Learning Objectives:
- to gain experience connecting different materials
- to better understand properties of materials
- to foster a community of collaboration and idea sharing

Materials: You can assign different pairs of students different materials if you'd like them to compare and contrast materials during discussions.
- scissors
- hair dryer or fan
- spray bottle
- cardboard
- paper
- masking tape
- duct tape
- glue gun
- paper clips
- clay
- LEGO bricks
- pipe cleaners
- popsicle sticks
- duct tape
- tin foil
- plastic wrap

Directions:
1) Explain to students that they will build houses. Discuss design constraints (materials in room, time, etc.) and criteria (e.g., must have standard house features such as a door and windows, must be sturdy enough to withstand a storm [hair dryer and spray bottle of water]). Let students know that you will ask them to share any useful building techniques with the rest of the class.
2) Show the students the materials they can choose from OR assign each group materials.

3) Students can sketch their initial designs. Once they have a sketch, they can begin building.
4) About fifteen minutes into building, have the students come together to share their building techniques.
5) Have students return to building and finish.
6) Make sure you leave time to have a final discussion with the class and to test their designs.

Possible Discussion Topics:
- ◆ Were there materials that were harder or easier to work with than you thought they would be?
- ◆ What were the pro and cons of different materials?
- ◆ Which materials were best for sturdy structures?
- ◆ What building techniques did you use? Did you find a way to attach materials to each other that you think worked well? Which materials are best for connecting?
- ◆ Did you see something that someone else did that you thought would be helpful to you?

Appendix N
Chair for a Bear

Lesson Overview: Students must create a chair for a stuffed bear or other animal that is approximately 12" tall. The chair should be sturdy and support the stuffed animal as it sits and be personalized for the stuffed animal. It should not slump over.

Suggested Time: 60–90 minutes

Learning Objectives:
- to get experience incorporating constraints and criteria into planning for a client
- to gain experience testing and iterating
- to understand the concept of sturdy building

Materials:
Interlocking building bricks, recycled and craft materials, or a combination
- interlocking building bricks
- cardboard
- paper
- tape
- paperclips
- string
- binder clips
- pipe cleaners
- popsicle sticks
- paper cups

Directions:
1) Explain that the engineering problem is to create a sturdy chair to support a stuffed animal. The chair must be able to hold up the stuffed animal and prevent it from falling out of the seat. The chairs must also be able to survive the drop test when dropped from their ankles. If different groups are using different stuffed animals, discuss how chair designs should accommodate the needs of each stuffed animal.
2) Show the students pictures of different chair designs and discuss the benefits of one chair to another.
3) Students begin by sketching their ideas for chairs. Have them label the pieces they think they will be using.

4) After they have sketched out an idea, they can begin building.

5) After ten minutes, stop for a mid-design share-out. Talk about what each group is going to do next and if they have already tested. Groups can share helpful building tips with each other.

6) Students should continue building.

7) Gather students to start testing their chairs; if a chair breaks or does not support Mr. Bear, they should improve their design and test it a second time. Students can also drop their chairs from their ankles to test for sturdiness.

8) Give students time to iterate.

9) Conclude the lesson by reviewing the methods of constructing a sturdy chair.

Possible Discussion Topics:
- What special considerations will your specific animal need? How will you serve this animal's needs with your chair?
- Did the animal fit in the chair?
- Did the animal stay upright or flop over?
- Did the animal look relaxed or straight?
- Did the animal's legs dangle or was there support for the legs?

Appendix O
Stomp Rocket

Lesson Overview: Students will create a paper stomp rocket that carries a specified payload to a specified target.

Suggested Time: 60–120 minutes

Design Criteria: The rocket will reach the target destination, carrying the specified payload (each group had a different, randomly assigned payload and target)

Learning Objectives:
- to build collective knowledge of rocket design
- to gain experience evaluating tests results to make design changes

Materials:
- paper
- foam sheets
- transparencies
- card stock
- tape—ideally different types
- paper clips
- small paper cups
- cone-shaped small paper cups
- weight—washers or coins work well
- optional: a wooden dowel the same diameter as the launcher to help students roll their paper into the correctly sized tube

For the Testing Station:
- inexpensive commercially available plastic rocket launchers
- printed targets (planets, moons, space station, etc.)

Directions:
- Set up the launcher on one end of a room and tape the printed targets to the floor in a line going away from the launcher.
- Give each student group a mission to carry a certain amount of weight to a certain target. To avoid competition, it can be helpful to give each group a different mission, with more weight for the closer targets.
- Show students how the launcher works: A rocket will slide on top of the plastic tube, then someone stomps or jumps on the soft plastic balloon part to launch the rocket.

- You may want to show students images of different kinds of real rockets, so they do not fixate on common cartoon images of rockets.
- Have small groups begin working on and testing their designs. Most designs have a body made of paper, foam sheet, or transparency rolled up and secured with a cup secured on the top. If students have trouble rolling their rockets to the right size for the launcher, provide them with dowels the same diameter as the launcher for them to use while building.

Possible Discussion Topics:
- Students can share advice about different problems they've faced, such as the rocket tops flying off during testing, weight falling off, or rockets staying stuck on the launcher.
- As the designs in this task are usually very similar, it provides a great sense-making opportunity across designs. Students can look across designs and think about what factors matter the most in how far a rocket travels and how much weight it can hold. Students often think first about how heavy a design is but later come to notice that the shape, materials, weight distribution, and cup type all matter as well.

Appendix P
Novel Engineering: Peter's Chair

Lesson Overview: This activity is based on the book *Peter's Chair* by Ezra Jack Keats. The class will need to read the book to do the activity. Although the book is for early elementary students, it has been used with older grades with less focus on literacy.

Suggested Time: 45–120 minutes, depending on ages of students

Students will pick a problem from the story and design a solution to solve a problem for one or more of the characters.

Learning Objectives:
- to gain experience identifying problems
- to gain experience problem scoping
- to design a solution for a client based on criteria and constraints that have been identified

Materials:
- scissors

Recyclable Materials:
- thin cardboard (like cereal box thickness)
- old magazines
- paper towel rolls
- empty small plastic containers such as yogurt containers
- empty water bottles

Purchased Materials:
- tape (masking seems to work the best)
- foil
- popsicle sticks
- felt or fabric
- plastic wrap
- string
- pipe cleaners
- paper clips
- coffee filters

Directions:
1) Read the book with the students. Tell them that they will build a solution to solve a problem for one of the characters. Have them keep a list of problems they find as they read. For younger students, stop at each page and discuss what is happening in the picture. For older students, remind them to look at the images for information about the characters. As you read, ask the students to share what they think the different characters are feeling at different times in the story.
2) As a group, list the problems that the students found on an anchor chart. Talk about which problems could be solved with engineering and which are more social. For example, students could build quieter blocks through engineering.
3) Pick one of the problems and talk about how that problem affects each member of the family. Talk about constraints and criteria in the story. Brainstorm possible solutions.
4) Tell students that they will pick a problem, design and then build an engineering solution to solve that problem. Introduce students to the materials.
5) Put students into pairs and have each pair pick a problem.
6) Have students brainstorm possible solutions and then begin planning using a planning document. Make sure they outline the constraints, criteria, and how they will test their design.
7) Students can begin building.
8) Stop for a mid-design share-out after students have built something, but still have work to do. Use the mid-design share-out for students to share what is working well and what they are trying to figure out. Have groups share advice with each other.
9) Students continue to build and test.
10) Students can share their designs through a presentation and/or another method such as an advertisement for the device.

Possible Discussion Topics:
◆ What about your design works well?
◆ What would you like help with?
◆ How will this solve the problem for your character(s)?
◆ How would the characters use it?

Appendix Q
Abby the Dog

Lesson Overview: This activity is based on a case study from the Tufts School of Veterinary Medicine about a dog named Abby who has mobility issues in her back legs. Abby is no longer able to do the things she used to do so students will build something that will improve Abby's life while keeping her injured lower back safe.

Suggested Time: 60–120 minutes

Learning Objectives:
- ◆ to get experience planning for a client
- ◆ to incorporating constraints and criteria
- ◆ to make connections between engineering and real-life situations

Materials:
- ◆ scissors
- ◆ felt or fabric
- ◆ stuffed dachshund
- ◆ wheels
- ◆ cardboard
- ◆ paper
- ◆ tape
- ◆ paperclips
- ◆ wire
- ◆ velcro
- ◆ string
- ◆ binder clips
- ◆ pipe cleaners
- ◆ popsicle sticks
- ◆ paper cups

Directions:
1) Let students know that they will be building something to help a dog whose back legs are temporarily unusable.
2) Introduce Abby. Abby is an 8-year-old female dachshund who is fond of playing ball and jumping on and off the couch in her owner's den. One morning, Abby wasn't acting like herself and seemed very reluctant to get up from her bed to move around the room.

When she did walk, she had a funny stilted gait that some describe as "walking on eggshells." By the time the owners were able to take Abby to the veterinarian later that morning, she was unable to stand and was partially paralyzed in both of her rear legs.

Findings from a thorough neurological exam and radiographs suggested that Abby had ruptured an intervertebral disc and that the contents had damaged her spinal cord. After surgery, Abby still couldn't walk and so the veterinarian suggested that some kind of device was needed to help Abby in her day-to-day life until she healed. The veterinarian felt that Abby would improve but would still need help moving for several weeks to come.

Abby is now not able to do the following things:
- Jumping on the bed
- Chasing the ball
- Walking to food
- Walking with the owner
- Swimming
- Running
- Playing games with other dogs
- Dig with her back legs

Requirements for the assistive technology:
- Has to be comfortable on Abby: not too tight or too loose
- Easily attached and removed
- Takes very little time to put on/off
- Nothing can be glued, taped, pinned, etc. to Abby
- Must support the lower back and legs
- Lower back and hips must be kept as still and stable as possible when the device is being used

3) After understanding the challenges faced by Abby, lead two brainstorming discussions. Focus the first one on Abby's day-to-day problems. Focus the second one on building ideas and constraints (size, weight and cost, etc), weight, cost, etc). Be sure to document the ideas in a visible location for reference. If not mentioned previously, discuss fit, stability, and ease of taking the device on and off.

4) Students break into groups and begin planning. They should choose a problem together first and then take time to quietly draw or write about possible solutions to that problem. Once they have had some time to think on their own (2 minutes), they can brainstorm together and establish a single design plan with which to proceed. It is a good

idea to have an educator check their idea before they start building to make sure it is feasible.

5) Have students build and test their designs on the stuffed dog. Once their designs have been approved, students can grab materials that they need and begin to build.

6) Stop for a mid-design check-in.

7) Give students time to iterate on their designs based on the feedback from the check-in.

8) After students complete their designs, have them share again or facilitate a discussion that helps them reflect on the process.

Possible Discussion Topics:
- What problem did you choose?
- What did you build to solve it and why?
- What evidence did you use to help make design decisions?
- What changes did you make because of the feedback you got and your tests?
- What are you going to change about your design? What is your next step?

Appendix R
Back Scratcher

Lesson Overview: Students will build something to scratch their or another student's back.

Suggested Time: 45–60 minutes

Learning Objectives:
- to get experience testing and iterating
- to build with criteria in mind
- to understand how to connect different materials

Materials:
- interlocking building bricks and/or
- cardboard
- paper
- masking tape
- paperclips
- string
- straws
- pipe cleaners
- popsicle sticks
- paper towel tubes

Directions:
1) Tell the students they will engineer a solution to solve the problem of an itchy back. Discuss criteria for a successful design which should include:
   a) Does this design satisfy an itchy back?
   b) Can it be used without it falling apart?
2) Have students work in teams to brainstorm and figure out how to solve the problem of an itchy back. Encourage creativity reminding students that designs may differ even though they are all solving the same problem.
3) This activity does not require intricate planning, but have students sketch their ideas and label the different materials they would like to use.
4) After students have formulated a plan, allow them to build their ideas in teams using the available materials. Ask them how they will know when their design is finished and works.
5) Allow students to share their ideas and designs to get feedback from peers, keeping in mind the design's ability to solve the problem and meet the criteria for success.

6) Give students five minutes to use the information gained from testing and the feedback to improve their designs.
7) Students can share final designs by showing the group how they work, designing an advertisement, or another activity that meets classroom goals.

Appendix S
Exploring Circuits

Lesson Overview: Students will learn about circuits and simple electronics as they build an alarm. The activity can be expanded by doing the Lunchbox Alarm during the next session.

Suggested Time: 30–45 minutes

Learning Objectives:
- ◆ to learn about simple circuits
- ◆ to incorporate circuits into a design

Materials: This activity will work with different electronic kits and with basic electronic pieces if they include:
- ◆ 1.5-volt light bulbs
- ◆ buzzers
- ◆ AA Batteries
- ◆ AA Battery Holders with leads
- ◆ aluminum Foil
- ◆ non-conductive ribbon, fabric, or paper

Directions:
1) Introduce students to materials (except for buzzer)
2) Launching Question:
    a) How can we use this battery to light up this bulb?
3) Encourage students to find different ways to make the bulb light up.
4) Document students' successful and unsuccessful attempts on chart paper or in slide show.
5) Lead a discussion interpreting the results—What do we need to light up the bulb?
    a) Focus on circuit ideas:
        i) a complete path
        ii) conductive materials (using aluminum foil, using battery holder)
6) Introduce vocabulary and diagrams relevant to your goals (e.g., electricity, electrons, etc.).
7) Introduce buzzer and discuss how it might work like bulbs.
8) Introduce challenge—Students that will create a circuit that is part of an alarm system.
9) Have students draw their plan.

10) As students build their circuits, they will likely vary from what they drew.
11) Students can test each other's alarms.
12) When students finish, have them share what they learned about how to work with the buzzer.
13) Final discussions can also focus on what they think they will need to incorporate the materials as a lunchbox alarm.

Appendix T
Art Bot (Robotics)

Lesson Overview: Students will create a robotic artist. Students can either create a robot that will create a piece of art, choosing their medium and style of robot, OR all students can build a spin art robot.

Suggested Time: 60 minutes

Learning Objectives:
- to gain an understanding of gearing
- to coordinate building and programming a robot
- to gain experience building a system

Materials:
- robotics kits
- gears (optional)
- cardboard
- paper
- tape
- paint
- paint brushes
- markers

Directions:
1) As a whole group, share examples of different types and mediums of art. You can stipulate constraints for the robot. For example, it must contain gears and sensors.
2) Tell students they will build a robot to help them create art. Show them the material selection for the art. They should be familiar with the robotic materials at this point.
3) Put students in groups. Have them pick what they will use for the art materials and canvas (size, material, etc.).
4) Have students use a planning document to plan the robot. They should label the parts. They should also address how the paintbrush or markers will be attached to the robot and where the medium will be attached.
5) Once the students have a plan, they can begin building. Remind them to test as they go.
6) The final share can be a showcase of the art that the students create.

Appendix U
Miniature Golf Course (Robotics)

Lesson Overview: Each group of students designs a miniature golf obstacle so that when they are put in a series, they have created a miniature golf course. Although the mechanisms will be robotic, students can use other types of materials for the obstacle. You can stipulate if you want students to include gears and sensors.

Suggested Time: 140–180 minutes

Learning Objectives:
- to coordinate building and programming a robot
- to gain experience building a system
- to collaborate to build a system

Materials:
- scissors
- golf balls
- golf club, putter
- paper cup or something else as the hole
- interlocking building bricks
- cardboard
- paper
- tape
- paperclips
- string
- binder clips
- pipe cleaners
- popsicle sticks
- paper cups

Directions:
1) Talk about and show pictures of mini golf obstacles. Discuss which kinds of obstacles are feasible to build using the robotics materials in the classroom. This conversation can include methods of movement for the obstacles (swinging, spinning, etc.).
2) Have students coordinate the order of the obstacles so each group knows when their obstacle will fall in the order.
3) Give students time to plan their obstacle.
4) Check students' plans before they begin to build.
5) Students build their mini golf obstacles.

Optional:

The students can program their obstacle to play a victory noise when the ball gets to the hole, or something totally different.

◆ Students can build putters.

◆ Students can add a theme for each hole and add decorations based on that theme.

Appendix V
Silly Walks (Robotics)

Lesson Overview: In this activity, students will build a robot that can move without the use of wheels. This can be achieved with very little or no programming experience. The motors just need to move forward.

Suggested Time: 45–60 minutes

Learning Objectives:
- ◆ to understand simple programming (move forward)
- ◆ to practice building with robotics components
- ◆ to be able to think outside of the box of nontraditional ways to make the robot move (NO CARS!)

Materials:
- ◆ robotics kit that includes a variety of building pieces
- ◆ motors

Directions:
1) Show students how the motors work, indicating which part spins and what parts are used to attach to the brick. The motors must be physically attached to the brick to move.
2) Before students build the silly walker, have them explore the materials and share two different ways they can attach the motors.
3) Students can build the silly walkers, testing as they work.
4) Give students a five- to ten-minute warning to complete their robots.
5) Have the students put all the robots down on the floor and start them all at once. All motors should be programmed to move forward.

Possible Discussion Topics:
- ◆ What was easy about this activity?
- ◆ What was challenging about this activity?
- ◆ What is a tip you want to share with others about building?
- ◆ What would you have done differently?

Appendix W
Biomimetics (Robotics)

Lesson Overview: Students will build a robotic device that emulates an animal's digging movements.

Suggested Time: 120 minutes

Learning Objectives:
- to research and analyze the structure and function of digging animals
- to build a robot that will mimic the movement of an animal
- to build coordinate building and programming for a robot

Materials:
- robotics kit including motors
- cardboard
- tape
- paperclips
- binder clips
- pipe cleaners
- popsicle sticks

Testing Station:
- shoeboxes or plastic tubs of a similar size
- shredded paper, cotton balls, or wood chips

Directions:
1) Tell students they will build and program a robot that will mimic a digging animal. The robot will dig shredded paper, cotton balls, or wood chips. Show the students the testing stations that have the boxes filled with the materials.
2) Facilitate a conversation with students as you talk about different animals that dig and how they dig (e.g., claws, teeth, tail). During this discussion, look at images of animals that dig and their skeletal systems.
3) Next, have each group pick the animal that they want to emulate. Share the materials they will use so they can begin planning. Students may want to spend time researching their animal and how it digs.
4) Have students complete planning sheets that include a drawing of their intended device.

5) While students build their robots, remind them to program and test as they work. Optional: Tests can include how much the robots can dig in a specified amount of time.

6) As part of the mid-design share-out, have students test their designs and give each other feedback.

7) Be sure that students iterate on their designs based on feedback.

8) At the end, ask students to show how their digger works and/or create a poster of the digger and images of animals.

Possible Discussion Topics:

◆ How does your animal dig?

◆ How did you mimic your animal's motion?

◆ How is the motion like your animal? How is it different?

◆ What other materials would you need to make your robot more accurate?

Appendix X
Lunch Box Protector (Alarm)

Lesson Overview: Students will build something to protect lunch that is kept in a lunch box.

Suggested Time: 60–90 minutes

Learning Objectives:
- ◆ to practice using sensors
- ◆ to practice building with robotics components

Materials:

Testing Stations:
- ◆ lunchboxes

Building:
- ◆ robotics building materials (students may want to incorporate sounds or lights as part of their designs)
- ◆ motors
- ◆ sensors
- ◆ cardboard
- ◆ paper
- ◆ tape
- ◆ paperclips
- ◆ string
- ◆ binder clips
- ◆ pipe cleaners
- ◆ popsicle sticks

Directions:
1) Tell students they will build a lunch box protector for a student whose lunch is regularly being stolen. They can use a variety of materials but must use at least one sensor. Discuss design constraints and criteria. Be sure to mention that the device cannot harm anyone.
2) Have students work in pairs or small groups. They should begin by using a planning document. Students should have access to the lunch boxes so they can test as they build.
3) Have students program and build as they work. They do not need to complete one task before moving on to the other task.

4) Stop for a mid-design share-out to get feedback from classmates and offer tips to each other.
5) Give students time to iterate on their designs.
6) For a final share-out, students can test each other's devices and try to break into them.

Possible Discussion Topics:
- ◆ What were the different designs you discussed at the beginning?
- ◆ Why did you choose the design you chose?
- ◆ Do you have any programming tips for the group?

Appendix Y
Longer/Final Project Trajectory

Lesson Overview: Longer projects in the book include an amusement park ride (robotics), a game for a younger student, an improvement for the classroom or school, and a miniature golf course where each group builds a different obstacle.

Suggested Time: We give a seven-session trajectory for longer projects with sixty minutes per session. This is variable depending on the amount of time you have and what your goals are.

Learning Objectives:
- to manage working through the engineering design process
- to choose a problem
- to outline design constraints and criteria

Materials:
- robotics kits (optional)
- craft, recyclable, and office materials

Directions:

Day	Sub-Activity	Notes
1	Introduce Challenge & Problem Scoping	Students begin filling in their planning document as they scope the problem.
2	Research, Brainstorm, Planning	Students continue to fill in the planning worksheet, manipulating materials as needed.
3	Build	Students test as they build. These may be mini tests of components or tests to see how their designs work overall. Students will iterate as they test and document as they work.
4	Mid-Design Share-out & Building	Students continue to test, iterate, and document. During this session, they also share their designs as part of a whole-class discussion or groups are paired with one other group to share their designs.

Day	Sub-Activity	Notes
5	Build	Students continue to build, test, iterate, and document.
6	Final Share-Out	Students share their final designs. Teachers should choose the option that aligns with their classroom goals. Example includes presenting a final presentation, writing a missing chapter for the book, and creating a poster that highlights how their design will work and how it will help the characters.
7	Clean-up and Reflection	Reflection may be included as part of documentation and/or through class discussion. It can include personal reflections on the process and/or lessons learned about topics such as materials and collaboration.

Supporting Content

Appendix Z
Website Links

1) Tufts University Center for Engineering Education and Outreach: ceeo.tufts.edu
2) Additional Book-Specific Content: introducingengineering.com
3) Engineering Design Talks: engineeringdesigntalks.org
4) ConnecTions: go.tufts.edu/connections
5) Drexel University ExCITe Center: drexel.edu/excite/innovation/illest/
6) Novel Engineering: novelengineering.org